MW00436905

SIGNS AND WONDERS

AT A GLANCE

Serendipity House / P.O. Box 1012 / Littleton, CO 80160

TOLL FREE 1-800-525-9563 / www.serendipityhouse.com

©1998 Serendipity House. All rights reserved.

99 00 01 02 / **301 series** • **CHG** / 5 4 3 2

PROJECT ENGINEER:
Lyman Coleman

WRITING TEAM:
Richard Peace, Lyman Coleman, Andrew Sloan, Cathy Tardif

PRODUCTION TEAM:
Christopher Werner, Sharon Penington, Erika Tiepel

COVER PHOTO:
© Paul and Lindamarie Ambrose / FPG International LLC.

CORE VALUES

Community: The purpose of this curriculum is to build community within the body of believers around Jesus Christ.

Group Process: To build community, the curriculum must be designed to take a group through a step-by-step process of sharing your story with one another.

Interactive Bible Study: To share your "story," the approach to Scripture in the curriculum needs to be open-ended and right brain—to "level the playing field" and encourage everyone to share.

Developmental Stages: To provide a healthy program in the life cycle of a group, the curriculum needs to offer courses on three levels of commitment: (1) Beginner Stage—low-level entry, high structure, to level the playing field; (2) Growth Stage—deeper Bible study, flexible structure, to encourage group accountability; (3) Discipleship Stage—in-depth Bible study, open structure, to move the group into high gear.

Target Audiences: To build community throughout the culture of the church, the curriculum needs to be flexible, adaptable and transferable into the structure of the average church.

ACKNOWLEDGMENTS

To Zondervan Bible Publishers
for permission to use
the NIV text,
The Holy Bible, New International Bible Society.
© 1973, 1978, 1984 by International Bible Society.
Used by permission of Zondervan Bible Publishers.

WELCOME TO THE SERENDIPITY 301 DEPTH BIBLE STUDY SERIES

You are about to embark on an adventure into the powerful experience of depth Bible Study. The Serendipity 301 series combines three basic elements to produce a life-changing and group-changing course.

First, you will be challenged and enriched by the personal Bible Study that begins each unit. You will have the opportunity to dig into Scripture both for understanding and personal reflection. Although some groups may choose to do this section together at their meeting, doing it beforehand will greatly add to the experience of the course.

Second, you will benefit from the group sessions. Wonderful things happen when a small group of people get together and share their lives around the Word of God. Not only will you have a chance to take your personal study to a deeper level, you will have an opportunity to share on a deep level what's happening in your life and receive the encouragement and prayer support of your group.

Third, the 301 courses provide the stimulus and tools for your group to take steps toward fulfilling your group mission. Whether or not your group has gone through the preparation of a Serendipity 101 and 201 course, you can profit from this mission emphasis. The 32-page center section of this book will guide you through this process. And questions in the closing section of the group agenda will prompt your group to act upon the mission challenge to "give birth" to a new small group.

Put these three components together, and you have a journey in Christian discipleship well worth the effort. Enjoy God's Word! Enjoy genuine Christian community! Enjoy dreaming about your mission!

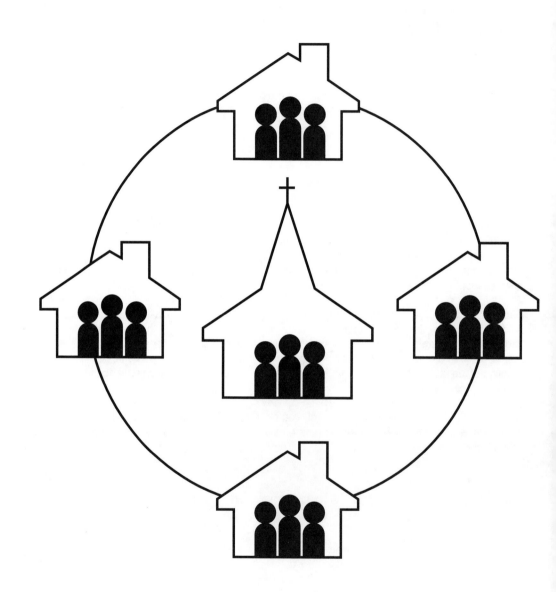

QUESTIONS & ANSWERS

STAGE

1. What stage in the life cycle of a small group is this course designed for?

Turn to the first page of the center section of this book. There you will see that this 301 course is designed for the third stage of a small group. In the Serendipity "Game Plan" for the multiplication of small groups, your group is in the Release Stage.

GOALS

2. What are the goals of a 301 study course?

As shown on the second page of the center section (page M2), the focus in this third stage is heavy on Bible Study and Mission.

BIBLE STUDY

3. What is the approach to Bible Study in this course?

This course involves two types of Bible Study. The "homework" assignment fosters growth in personal Bible study skills and in personal spiritual growth. The group study gives everyone a chance to share their learning and together take it to a deeper level.

SELF STUDY

4. What does the homework involve?

There are three parts to each assignment: (1) READ—to get the "bird's-eye view" of the passage and record your first impressions; (2) SEARCH—to get the "worm's-eye view" by digging into the passage verse-by-verse with specific questions; and (3) APPLY—to ask yourself, after studying the passage, "What am I going to do about it?"

THREE-STAGE LIFE CYCLE OF A GROUP

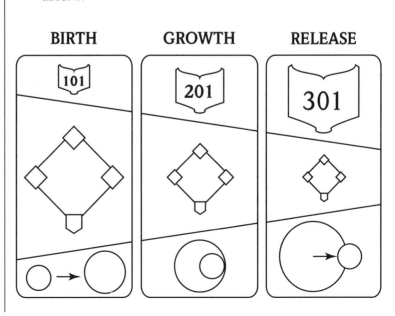

BIRTH GROWTH RELEASE

BIBLE KNOWLEDGE

5. *What if you don't know very much about the Bible?*

No problem. The homework assignment is designed to lead you step-by-step in your study. And there are study notes in each unit to give you help with key words, concepts and difficult passages.

AGENDA

6. *What is the agenda for the group meetings?*

The completed homework assignment becomes the basis for the group sharing. (However, those who don't do the homework should definitely be encouraged to come to the meeting anyway.) During the meeting the group will be guided to share on three levels: (1) TO BEGIN; (2) TO GO DEEPER; and (3) TO CLOSE.

STAYING ON TRACK

7. *How can the group get through all the material?*

Following the recommended time limits for each of the three sections will help keep you on track. Since you may not be able to answer all the questions with the time you have, you may need to skip some of them. Also, if you have more than seven people at a meeting, use the "Fearless Foursomes" described below for the Bible Study.

THE FEARLESS FOURSOME!

If you have more than seven people at a meeting, Serendipity recommends you divide into groups of 4 for the Bible Study. Count off around the group: "one, two, one, two, etc."—and have the "ones" move quickly to another room for the Bible Study. Ask one person to be the leader and follow the directions for the Bible Study time. After 30 minutes, the Group Leader will call "Time" and ask all groups to come together for the Caring Time.

GROUP BUILDING

8. *How does this course develop Group Building?*

Although this series is Serendipity's deepest Bible Study curriculum, Group Building is still essential. The group will continue "checking in" with each other and will challenge each other to grow in Christian discipleship. Working together on the group's mission should also be a very positive group-building process.

**MISSION /
MULTIPLICATION**

9. *What is the mission of a 301 group?*

Page M3 of the center section summarizes the mission of groups using this course: to commission a team from your group to start a new group. The center section will lead your group in doing this.

**LEADERSHIP
TRAINING**

10. *How do we incorporate this mission into the course?*

Page M5 of the center section gives an overview of the six steps in this process. You can either add this leadership training to the sessions a little bit at a time or in a couple of separate sessions.

**GROUP
COVENANT**

11. *What is a group covenant?*

A group covenant is a "contract" that spells out your expectations and the ground rules for your group. It's very important that your group discuss these issues—preferably as part of the first session.

**GROUND
RULES**

12. *What are the ground rules for the group?* (Check those that you agree upon.)

❒ PRIORITY: While you are in the course, you give the group meetings priority.

❒ PARTICIPATION: Everyone participates and no one dominates.

❒ RESPECT: Everyone is given the right to their own opinion and all questions are encouraged and respected.

❒ CONFIDENTIALITY: Anything that is said in the meeting is never repeated outside the meeting.

❒ EMPTY CHAIR: The group stays open to new people at every meeting as long as they understand the ground rules.

❒ SUPPORT: Permission is given to call upon each other in time of need—even in the middle of the night.

❒ ADVICE GIVING: Unsolicited advice is not allowed.

❒ MISSION: We agree to do everything in our power to start a new group as our mission (see center section).

INTRODUCTION TO MIRACLES

What Is a Miracle?

"I can't believe she said 'Yes!' It's a miracle, but I'm going to marry her!"

"The 1980 USA Olympic Hockey Team was a miracle team, winning the gold medal when no one thought they would be able to do it."

"The fact that he could survive such a fall is a miracle."

"I never thought I could win the mega-bucks. It's a miracle!"

For a society that is by and large skeptical of the supernatural, we still attribute a great number of things to the realm of the miraculous! However, such diversity in the way this word is used forces us to ask the question, "Just what do we mean when we call something a miracle?"

Behind each of the examples of the way the word "miracle" is used today lies the concept of an unexpected, tremendously beneficial event. God is not even necessarily involved; *any* stroke of unexpected good fortune is called a miracle. While the chances that any particular individual will win the mega-bucks are tiny, that *someone* will eventually win is simply a matter of the law of probability. None of the commentators who spoke of the 1980 USA Olympic hockey team's "miraculous" win of the gold medal would claim that God had somehow intervened, allowing USA shots to veer from normal angles of play to somehow find their way into the goal while mysteriously causing the opponents' shots to miss their mark. The survival of a person after a great fall, while indeed rare and unexpected, does not require the intervention of God to be explained. Reflecting this common use of the word "miracle," Roget's Thesaurus suggests the following words as possible synonyms: a marvel, a godsend, a serendipity, a bonanza, a spectacle, a boon, a windfall. Obviously, such an understanding of the miraculous does not adequately capture the meaning of the miracles in the Bible, and specifically in the ministry of Jesus. In the Bible, miracles are not simply a matter of good fortune, but an example of the presence of God.

Common Ideas About the Biblical Miracles

Everyone knows that the Bible tells of many miracles. The Old Testament records a host of miracle stories from the crossing of the Red Sea (Ex. 14), to floating axheads (2 Kings 6), to the defeat of the Assyrian army when it was about to destroy Jerusalem (2 Chron. 32). The New Testament begins with the miracle story about the virgin birth of Jesus, and the whole of Jesus' ministry is accompanied by a variety of actions termed miracles. The apostles in Acts, likewise, are credited with the ability to perform miracles such as healings and the raising of the dead.

Popularly, it is thought that the biblical miracles are events that happen contrary to nature. Indeed, there *are* stories of how God altered natural forces. The Red Sea was divided by a great wind. Severe plagues afflicted the Egyptians but spared the Israelites. Elijah was able to provide for the needs of a poor widow through the never-emptying flask of oil and always full jar of flour. Elisha made an axhead float. Jesus walked on water, silenced a storm by a single command, fed the five thousand with a few loaves of bread and a couple of fish, and turned water into wine at a wedding for the enjoyment of the guests. Elijah, Elisha, Jesus, Peter and Paul all raised at least one dead person to life. These accounts do require an overruling or a suspension of what we call natural laws. However, there are other types of miracles stories as well which do not necessarily involve actions contrary to nature.

For instance, there are many cases of healing. In these stories sick people recover immediately. While some of the healings were of people who otherwise would have died of their illness, other healings simply speeded up the normal recovery process. Jesus healed many blind or lame people, but recovery from blindness and paralysis is attested in modern times as well in cases of psychosomatic reactions to trauma.

There are also miracles of decisive victory over forces of entrenched evil. These are particularly true of Jesus' exorcism of demons. Other people in Jesus' day (and before and since) have demonstrated such abilities as well.

Finally, there are instances of the foreknowledge of events. The fact that Peter caught a fish with a coin in its mouth is not all that remarkable in itself. What is remarkable is that Jesus told him it would happen (Matt. 17:27)! However, many people would argue that instances of clairvoyance are not unique to Jesus.

From this survey, we can see that the miracles in the Bible come in a variety of forms. They do not necessarily involve exceptions to what we commonly know as the natural order of things. As we shall see, their distinctiveness lies elsewhere.

Another common opinion about the miracles of the Bible is that they are simply meant to authenticate the authority of the one who performs them. While this was true in some cases (as when Moses was allowed to perform certain miraculous acts to prove to the Israelites that he had indeed been sent by God), such a view does not do justice to the miracles of Jesus. This approach tends to see miracles as God's seal of approval upon the message given by his messenger. They prove that the messenger is from God. It is true that the miracles pointed to the uniqueness of Jesus: "The miracle-worker Jesus is unlike anything in ordinary experience. He arouses amazement and wonder. Where he appears, a gap is made in the fabric of ordinary, everyday experience: 'We have never seen anything like this' (Mark 2:12)."[1] His actions led people to ponder his identity and the significance of his actions.

However, the miracles revealed God's presence and power only to those who saw with the eyes of faith. Jesus' miracles were interpreted in widely different ways. Although many people saw them as evidence of the presence of God, others viewed them as acts of Satan intended to deceive people (Matt. 12:22ff). As such, they do not *prove* Jesus' divine authority, but are pointers to it to those whose hearts and minds are open to him.

A major difficulty with the idea that the miracles were primarily meant to be proofs of Jesus' authority is that Jesus repudiated this view several times! He refused to follow Satan's suggestion to stage a miraculous deliverance to prove that he was the Son of God (Matt. 4:6–7). He refused to perform a miracle simply to satisfy Herod's curiosity (Luke 23:8). He rejected the Pharisees' request for a sign to authenticate his authority (Mark 8:11–12). Indeed, it was the miracles themselves that often produced intense conflict with established religious authorities. The religious establishment lived comfortably with healing cults (such as is referred to in John 5:1ff) and other people who possessed abilities to heal, but Jesus' miracles were seen as being in opposition to sacred traditions and laws. He healed on the Sabbath, and made claims to divine prerogatives (Mark 2:1–12; 3:1–5). These were crisis-producing actions which forced people to choose between him and the established traditions. Despite the miracles, many chose to stick with the traditions. It is especially interesting to note that, particularly in Mark's account, many of the miracles were performed in secret with express orders for the people involved *not* to tell anyone what happened lest Jesus be misunderstood. The miracles were not in themselves irresistible proofs of Jesus' deity.

The biggest problem with this view of the miracles, however, is that it makes them essentially unnecessary. Such a view means that in and of themselves the miracles have no inherent meaning. Instead, they become only wonders done to amaze the crowds and get them to listen to Jesus.

The Message of the Miracles

It is far more in accord with the nature of Jesus' miracles to see them as an essential part of his message. Jesus' message would not be the same apart from the miracles, for they are the physical demonstrations of the news he announced regarding the inbreaking of the kingdom of God. Without the miracles, Jesus would simply have been another prophet looking ahead to the coming of the kingdom. The healing of the blind, the lame, the leprous, and the deaf, as well as the raising of the dead and the proclamation of the good news of God's kingdom (Matt. 11:4–5), all together point to the truth that in Jesus the kingdom of God has indeed begun to break in upon the world.

The Gospel of John especially illustrates the importance of the miracles as being part and parcel of Jesus' message. This Gospel is built around seven miracle stories which it calls "signs." That very term reveals an important insight about the way John viewed the meaning of miracles. They are not simply stories of Jesus' amazing power meant to get people's attention, nor are they simply acts of compassion for those who benefit by them. Rather, they reveal the nature of his kingdom. Colin Brown makes an important observation in this regard when he writes: "[The miracles] are signs of God's kingly rule, the dawn of which Jesus announced in his proclamation ... the miracles are a foreshadowing and a promise of the coming universal redemption. ... Thus, the casting out of demons signals God's invasion into the realm of Satan and its final annihilation; the raising of the dead announces that death will be forever done away with; the healing of the sick bears witness to the cessation of all suffering; the miraculous provisions of food are foretokens of the end of all physical need; the stilling of the storm points forward to the complete victory over the powers of chaos which threaten the earth."[2]

In the same vein, Karl Barth notes, "What took place [in the miracles] were promises and ... anticipations of a ... kind of life in which there will be no more sorrow, tears, and crying, and where death as the last enemy will be no more."[3]

Seen in this way, the miracle stories of Jesus become important signs of what God's kingdom (as well as the King) is all about. They demonstrate God's opposition to disease, chaos, suffering and death. In Christ, God has come to free people from the power of these forces. The miracles are therefore glimpses of what the kingdom of God truly means. They reflect the values and truths for which God's people are to work and pray. They accent Jesus' authority over all forces that oppress humanity. Demons, sickness, nature, and death itself are subject to Jesus. His miracles imply an authority to which people must become subject and illustrate the presence of a kingdom in which people are invited to participate.

The Problem of Miracles Today
Many people struggle with the whole notion of miracles. While the miracles used to be seen as the proof of the Christian claims to truth, now many Christians consider the miracle stories as somewhat embarrassing relics that seem out of place with the modern world. They are seen as something like the relatives you hope your friends never meet: you can't deny they are part of your history, but you aren't quite sure how to explain their presence!

Such a concern stems from a worldview that gained prominence during the Enlightenment. Simply put, it has no place for the miraculous because it has no place for a God who acts in history. While the biblical authors believed in God's sovereignty over all events, people today are conditioned to think in terms of natural laws, cause and effect, and physical properties. If any credence at all is given to the supernatural, it is assumed that there is a clear division between matters of nature and matters of the spirit. While such a view might acknowledge that the spiritual dimension of life is important for a person's inner life, it would deny that there is any relationship between the spiritual realm and the "reality" of the natural world.

The worldview of the biblical authors, however, was not divided into separate watertight "sacred" and "secular" compartments. "Natural law" was simply not thought of at this time. Instead, they viewed *all* of life as under God's control *all* of the time. The coming of the spring rain was not seen as the result of a complex weather pattern but as the gift of God to replenish the earth. Thus, the miraculous was not seen as a breaking of some independent law of nature or as an absolutely unexplainable event apart from God's intervention, but as a demonstration of the special presence of God. The spiritual realm was seen to have great impact upon the physical.

In contrast, modern technological society views historical and physical events in the world as simply the product of natural forces. It assumes the world is a closed system of cause and effect which can be studied and understood. By its very definition, such an approach rules out the possibility of supernatural intervention. This view does not disprove the biblical miracles; it simply assumes such things could not happen and thus seeks alternative explanations of these accounts.

The real issue is a matter of faith. Either we believe, like the biblical writers, that there is a God who is free to intervene in his creation, or we believe that the world is a closed system of cause and effect through natural forces. Both positions begin with an assumption. It is not as though those who believe in the latter view have more information or insight than those who believe the former, nor does it imply that those who believe in the reality of miracles are somehow ignorant of the scientific discoveries of the past 400 years. Those who believe in miracles (whose number includes many scientists) simply see no compelling reason to rule out the possibility of God's intervention in what is called the "natural" world. They recognize that disbelief in the possibility of miracles is not a scientific position, but a philosophical commitment made for other reasons.

Can Miracles Happen Today?

In the Bible, miracles cluster around those times wherein God moves history toward its final goal in an especially powerful, significant way. "God does not shake miracles into Nature at random as if from a pepper-caster. They come on great occasions ... of that spiritual history which cannot be fully known by men (sic) ... ."[4] There are the dramatic stories of God's power associated with the Exodus and the conquest of the Promised Land, yet after that Israel went for centuries with only rare demonstrations of power. Elijah and Elisha, the first of the great prophets, performed miracles but Isaiah, Jeremiah and Ezekiel did not. By far, most of Israel's history was not marked by miracles. Spirituality was not a matter of having power to perform wondrous acts, but a matter of acting justly, loving mercy, and walking humbly with God (Micah 6:8).

The New Testament never calls upon Christians to "expect a miracle" to relieve them of the common pains of life or to convince doubters of the Gospel. Miracles like the water becoming wine, the feeding of the five thousand, and the raising of Lazarus were special, unique signs highlighting Jesus' identity and graphically depicting the nature of the life which he will give to all when the kingdom is fully revealed. The church today probably should not expect miracles such as these. These are miracles that were meant to anticipate what the final reality of God's people will be like, not a taste of what day-to-day life in Christ will bring.

But what about that boy whose leg was healed after prayer, or the cancer-ridden patient who was suddenly found to have no traces of the disease? How does one account for the softening of a hardhearted person such that they believe the Gospel? What about the strange circumstances that "just happened" so that a person was protected from some harm that otherwise would

have occurred? Such stories are frequent enough that many Christians believe that God still intervenes in miraculous ways, especially in the areas of healings, exorcisms and conversions.

The Scripture certainly encourages people to pray with the expectation that prayer makes a difference. The deist conception of the world as a clock created by a cosmic watchmaker that is then left to run on its own is neither a biblical understanding of God nor the world. The Scripture describes God as the Living God precisely because the writers believe that God acts in history. Thus, it is not for us to rule out the possibility of God's intervention at any time.

However, those who do not experience such dramatic acts must never feel they are second-class citizens of the kingdom. Most Christians throughout history have not seen a miracle. Fervent prayers for healing or deliverance from harm often go unanswered. If we believe God is free to intervene at any point for his purposes, we must also believe he is free from being controlled by human interests or desires. Instead, we must embrace the truth that God is free to act at any time, in any place, in any way, for his purposes and glory.

However, this should not be an excuse for a lazy faith that reflects more of the modern notion that God is separate and rather uninvolved in his creation than the biblical belief in the Living God. "The malady of our time lies in its contracted thoughts of God. We think too narrowly and meanly of His Power, His Love and His Freedom to help. ... That is what the miracles of Jesus and His teachings about faith mean ... God is more near, more real and mighty, more full of love, and more ready to help every one of us than any one of us realizes, that is [the miracles'] undying message."[5]

[1]Gerd Thiessen, *The Miracle Stories of the Early Christian Tradition*, T&T Clark, 1983, p. 301.
[2]Colin Brown (ed.), *Dictionary of New Testament Theology*, Vol. 11, *Miracle*.
[3]Karl Barth, *Evangelical Theology: An Introduction*, pp. 68-69.
[4]C.S. Lewis, *Miracles*, p. 174.
[5]D.S. Cairns, *The Faith That Rebels*, Richard Smith, Inc., 1930, pp. 246-247.

UNIT 1—Water Into Wine / John 2:1-11

Jesus Changes Water to Wine

2 On the third day a wedding took place at Cana in Galilee. Jesus' mother was there, ²and Jesus and his disciples had also been invited to the wedding. ³When the wine was gone, Jesus' mother said to him, "They have no more wine."

⁴Dear woman, why do you involve me?" Jesus replied. "My time has not yet come."

⁵His mother said to the servants, "Do whatever he tells you."

⁶Nearby stood six stone water jars, the kind used by the Jews for ceremonial washing, each holding from twenty to thirty gallons."[a]

⁷Jesus said to the servants, "Fill the jars with water"; so they filled them to the brim.

⁸Then he told them, "Now draw some out and take it to the master of the banquet."

They did so, ⁹and the master of the banquet tasted the water that had been turned into wine. He did not realize where it had come from, though the servants who had drawn the water knew. Then he called the bridegroom aside ¹⁰and said, "Everyone brings out the choice wine first and then the cheaper wine after the guests have had too much to drink; but you have saved the best till now."

¹¹This, the first of his miraculous signs, Jesus performed at Cana in Galilee. He thus revealed his glory, and his disciples put their faith in him.

[a]6 Greek [*two to three metretes*] (probably about 75 to 115 liters)

READ

Two readings of the passage are suggested—each with a response to be checked or filled in on the worksheet.

First Reading / First Impressions: How do you imagine Jesus felt about his mother's suggestion that he do something about the wine running out?

❏ annoyed   ❏ manipulated   ❏ reluctant
❏ embarrassed   ❏ honored   ❏ willing

Second Reading / Big Idea: This story only appears in this Gospel. What point might John have wanted to emphasize by including it?

SEARCH

1. Given the importance of social customs (see first note on v. 3), what do you suppose is going on in the kitchen behind the scenes?

2. What do you learn about Mary and Jesus from the interchange in verses 3–5? What is the meaning of his response to her (v. 4; see notes)?

3. Pretend you are one of the servants. Retell the story of verses 6–9 from your perspective as you might share it with your spouse when you went home that night.

4. What is the significance of the "new wine" and of the fact that the water changed into wine was from jars used for ceremonial cleansing (see notes on v. 6)?

5. While the master of the banquet was simply glad the party was not spoiled, what might John be wanting to show about Jesus' glory by using this as the first miracle in his Gospel?

6. What effect did this incident have on Jesus' new disciples (v. 11)?

APPLY

1. As you begin this course, what are some goals you would like to work on? Check one or two from the list below and add another if you wish.
   - ❏ to get to know God in a more personal way
   - ❏ to understand what I believe as a Christian and where I stand on issues
   - ❏ to develop my skills in Bible study and personal devotions
   - ❏ to belong to a small group that will support me in my growth
   - ❏ to think through my values and priorities in light of God's will
   - ❏ to wrestle with the next step in my spiritual journey with others who care

2. What are you willing to commit to in the way of disciplines during the time you are in this course?
   - ❏ to complete the Bible study home assignment before the group meets
   - ❏ to attend the group meetings except in cases of emergency
   - ❏ to share in leading the group—taking my turn in rotation
   - ❏ to keep confidential anything that is shared in the group
   - ❏ to reach out to others who are not in a group and invite them to join us
   - ❏ to participate in the group's mission of "giving birth" to a new group (see center section)

GROUP AGENDA

Every group meeting has three parts: (1) To Begin (10–15 minutes) to break the ice; (2) To Go Deeper (30 minutes) for Bible Study; and (3) To Close (15–30 minutes) for caring and prayer. When you get to the second part, have someone read the Scripture out loud and then divide into groups of 4 (4 at the dining table, 4 at the kitchen table, etc.). Then have everyone come back together for the third part.

TO BEGIN / 10–15 Min. (Choose 1 or 2)
1. What is the funniest thing that happened at a wedding you attended?

2. What is the most enjoyable or unusual wedding reception you have been to?

3. When was a time your mother embarrassed you in public?

TO GO DEEPER / 30 Min. (Choose 2 or 3)
1. Quickly go through as many of the READ and SEARCH homework questions as you have time to cover.

2. What do you think about Jesus and Mary's relationship based on this story?

3. What is meant by the word "sign" to describe this miracle?

4. What is the "wine" level (zest for living) in your life at the moment: Full? Half-full? Empty?

5. What is draining you? What area of your life feels like stale water in an old jug?

TO CLOSE / 15–30 Min.
1. What did you check under APPLY for the goals you would like to work on during this course?

2. What disciplines are you willing to commit to (second question in APPLY)?

3. How can the group help you in prayer this week?

NOTES

Summary. This incident is the first of seven signs around which chapters 2–12 of John's Gospel are built. These miracles (2:1–11; 4:43–54; 5:1–15; 6:1–13, 16–21; 9:1–11; 11:38–44) are specifically called "signs" because they are not simply acts of power, but are meant to demonstrate the glory of God in Jesus (John 1:14). They are presented so that the reader might share in the confession that "these (signs) are written that you may believe that Jesus is the Christ, the Son of God, and that by believing you may have life in his name" (John 20:31). In this story, the growing recognition of who Jesus is climaxes with the affirmation of the disciples' faith (v. 11).

2:1 *On the third day.* It has been observed that John's Gospel is an extended meditation on the meaning of Jesus' death and resurrection, since from the very beginning of the Gospel there are allusions to these events (i.e., "the Lamb of God" in 1:29; Jesus' reference to the destruction of his body and the resurrection in 2:19; the reference to Jesus being lifted up in 3:14). The reference here to the "third day" begs us to read this story in light of the reality of Christ's resurrection on the third day after his death. This story highlights both the new quality of life brought into being through Jesus' death and resurrection, and his intention to replace the formal religious structures of his day with the reality of joyful intimacy with God.

wedding. Weddings were important social events for the community; a time when all the relatives and townspeople would gather to celebrate, often for up to a week!

Cana. The exact location of this village (mentioned only here and in John 4:46) is unknown, but it is believed to have been near Nazareth.

2:2 *Jesus and his disciples.* According to John's chronology thus far, Jesus only has five disciples, all residents of the immediate area (1:35,40–41, 43–49).

2:3 *the wine was gone.* This was potentially a very humiliating social situation. It would reflect badly on the host as someone too miserly to provide adequate refreshments for the guests. It would be seen as a sign that the guests were really not welcome.

They have no more wine. Why Jesus' mother approached Jesus with this concern is unknown, since he had not previously done anything to make her expect he could solve the problem. It implies her awareness of his role as the divinely appointed ruler of Israel, and perhaps is an encouragement on her part to start acting the part!

2:4 _Dear woman._ Jesus uses the same term to address other women (Matt. 15:28; Luke 13:12). It is not a harsh term, but it is an unusual term for a son to use with his mother. "That Jesus calls Mary 'Woman' and not 'Mother' probably indicates that there is a new relationship between them as He enters on His public ministry" (Morris).

why do you involve me? This phrase typically points to a division between the people or parties involved (Matt. 8:29; Mark 1:24; Luke 8:28). Since the time for his messianic role is at hand, Jesus is making it clear that from now on no other loyalties and relationships will be allowed to dominate that agenda. Barclay translates this as "Lady, let me handle this in my own way."

My time has not yet come. John frequently uses phrases and words with double meanings. Here, this phrase appears to mean simply that it is not yet appropriate for him to act. However, the "time" or "hour" of Jesus in this Gospel (7:6,8,30; 8:20; 12:23,27; 13:1) has a theological meaning as well. It is used to refer to those moments when things happen "to and through Jesus which reveal his ... majesty and authority" (Brown), culminating in his crucifixion (16:32; 17:1). Jesus' response to Mary in this scene communicates that he will not operate on any other time frame nor for any other purpose than the one his Father has assigned him.

2:5 _Do whatever he tells you._ Again (see v. 3), the reason for Mary's confidence in pressing on with this concern is unknown. The phrase does serve to show that the initiative is left with Jesus.

2:6 _six stone water jars._ Although not required by the Law of Moses, by Jesus' day many Jews, in order to show their devotion to God, practiced purification rituals based on those required of the priests (Ex. 30:19–20; Mark 7:1–4). For instance, water would be poured over the hands of the guests prior to the meal. A large event like this wedding would require a great deal of water for such cleansing. The fact that it is these jars that are used implies that the old ways of ritual purification are going to be radically transformed by Jesus.

twenty to thirty gallons. The drinking of wine did not have the associations with alcoholism and alcohol abuse as it does so often today. The use of wine was a way of showing hospitality to guests, an expression of one's desire that others join in as celebrants at a happy occasion. Jesus' provision of such an ample amount of wine puts him in the place of a host, generously and graciously providing for his guests. This story enacts the parables about the bridegroom and the new wine found in Mark 2:19–20; 2:22. The new wine Jesus gives totally transforms the old water of a formalized religion into a relationship with God characterized by joy and abundance (see John 1:16). Feasting and the abundance of wine is a characteristic image used in the Old Testament to describe the joy of God's people who have experienced his deliverance (Isa. 25:6; 55:1–2). This celebration is to begin because of the presence of Jesus.

2:9 _the master of the banquet._ This appears to have been an honored guest at the wedding, serving in a role somewhat akin to that of a modern-day toastmaster.

He did not realize where it had come from. This parallels the theme throughout John's Gospel that the identity of Jesus is revealed only to those he chooses. Others see but do not comprehend.

he called the bridegroom. Weddings were typically held at the home of the groom or of his parents. The groom would be the one responsible for planning the wedding.

2:10 _Everyone brings out the choice wine first._ Typically, the best wine would be served when the guests would be most able to appreciate it. Later on, when they are less likely to notice, a cheaper quality of wine would be introduced. The quality of this wine was such that the master of the banquet thought the bridegroom had for some reason reversed the normal procedure.

2:11 _miraculous signs._ Although the other Gospels typically refer to Jesus' miracles with a word that lays the stress on their being works of power, John prefers to call them signs. This encourages his readers not to see these actions simply as the acts of a wonder worker, but as pointers to God's presence in Jesus, recognized by those who receive him (John 1:12). Likewise, they are physical and material illustrations of the spiritual life Jesus came to bring (see John 6:26–27; 9:1–5,39).

glory. While the master of the banquet failed to consider by whom the wine came, the disciples saw the reality behind the sign. This was their first glimpse of the light of God's glory manifested in Jesus.

UNIT 2—Jesus Drives Out an Evil Spirit / Mark 1:21-28

Jesus Drives Out an Evil Spirit

²¹They went to Capernaum, and when the Sabbath came, Jesus went into the synagogue and began to teach. ²²The people were amazed at his teaching, because he taught them as one who had authority, not as the teachers of the law. ²³Just then a man in their synagogue who was possessed by an evilᵃ spirit cried out, ²⁴"What do you want with us, Jesus of Nazareth? Have you come to destroy us? I know who you are—the Holy One of God!"

²⁵"Be quiet!" said Jesus sternly. "Come out of him!" ²⁶The evil spirit shook the man violently and came out of him with a shriek.

²⁷The people were all so amazed that they asked each other, "What is this? A new teaching—and with authority! He even gives orders to evil spirits and they obey him." ²⁸News about him spread quickly over the whole region of Galilee.

ᵃ23 Greek *unclean* ; also in verses 26 and 27

READ

First Reading / First Impressions: What comes to your mind when you think of stories in the Bible like this about evil spirits?

❒ curiosity   ❒ excitement   ❒ confusion

❒ fear   ❒ disgust   ❒ other:_____

Second Reading / Big Idea: What seems to be one or two key words in this passage?

SEARCH

1. What things are implied when it is said that Jesus taught with "authority" (see third note on v. 22)?

2. What emotions do you associate with the idea of being "amazed" (vv. 22,27)? What qualities in Jesus produced this reaction in the people (see first note on v. 22 and notes on v. 27)?

3. Since the demon correctly identified Jesus, why might Jesus have ordered it to "Be quiet!" (v. 25, see note)?

16

4. What effect did this miracle have on Jesus' ministry (v. 28)?

5. This is the first miracle recorded in Mark. What might he be wanting to show about Jesus in this initial demonstration of his power?

6. The miracles are not just isolated incidents, but signs of something greater that Jesus has come to do. If this was the only story of Jesus you knew so far, what insights about the kingdom of God would you be able to gain from it?

APPLY

1. Given your understanding and experience of Jesus to this point, what are a couple of things about him or his teaching that leave you "amazed"? Why?

2. Jesus used his authority to bring freedom and wholeness to this man. In what ways have you experienced Jesus' authority doing the same in your life? Is there an area that seems to be blocking you from such freedom now?

GROUP AGENDA

Every group meeting has three parts: (1) To Begin (10–15 minutes) to break the ice; (2) To Go Deeper (30 minutes) for Bible Study; and (3) To Close (15–30 minutes) for caring and prayer. When you get to the second part, have someone read the Scripture out loud and then divide into groups of 4 (4 at the dining table, 4 at the kitchen table, etc.). Then have everyone come back together for the third part.

TO BEGIN / 10–15 Min. (Choose 1 or 2)

1. Who was one of your best teachers? What made them such a good teacher?

2. Have you seen or known anyone who seemed to be possessed by an evil spirit?

3. How do you feel about Ouija boards, tarot cards, palm readers and horoscopes?

TO GO DEEPER / 30 Min. (Choose 2 or 3)

1. Have each person choose one of the questions in READ or SEARCH to answer.

2. What do you learn about demons from this episode in the synagogue? What do you learn about Jesus?

3. Do you think Christians can be "possessed" by an evil spirit and the Holy Spirit at the same time? Can they be attacked by an evil spirit? What protection do they have against such attacks?

4. What do you think about exorcism (casting out demons)?

5. CASE STUDY: Your friend Judy recently sought help for severe anxiety. A psychiatrist wants to prescribe medication, and a Christian known for having a "deliverance ministry" agrees with Judy's fears that her problems are demonic. What should Judy do?

TO CLOSE / 15–30 Min.

1. Who could you invite to this group next week?

2. Share your answer to at least one of the questions in APPLY.

3. On a scale from 1 (none) to 10 (total), how much authority do you allow Jesus Christ to have in your life? What would have to be "cast out" of your life to raise your rating to a 10?

4. How can the group pray for you?

NOTES

Summary. With his four newly chosen disciples present (Mark 1:16–20), Jesus' first public act of ministry recorded by Mark occurs in a synagogue. Here, with God's chosen people assembled, Jesus makes his presence known by the quality of his teaching and by his extraordinary power over demonic powers.

1:21 *Capernaum*. This was a town on the north end of the Sea of Galilee, three miles west of the River Jordan. It was a center of the fishing industry and the site of a custom's post.

***synagogue*.** In first-century Israel, the temple in Jerusalem was the sole site for sacrifices and was attended by numerous priests and other officials. In contrast, there were synagogues in each population center which people attended each week for worship and instruction. Synagogues were run by lay committees with no professional clergy attached to them. Anyone could speak as long as they had permission from the leaders.

1:22 *amazed*. Throughout the Gospel of Mark, Jesus' words and actions provoke amazements and surprise among the people. Neither his word nor his actions were customary—they could not be easily integrated with what went on day by day. Here was something new that challenged accepted ways of thinking and living. Jesus' words and actions were pointers to the kingdom he was establishing, a kingdom that called for a response of repentance and faith from those wishing to be part of it (Mark 1:15). Lane notes that Jesus' words and actions had a "more-than-prophetic note ... Jesus' word, presented with a sovereign authority which permitted neither debate nor theoretical reflection, confronted the congregation with the absolute claim of God upon their whole person. Jesus' teaching recalled the categorical demand of the prophets rather than scribal tradition."

***at his teaching*.** Mark records very little of Jesus' teaching in his Gospel. Essentially, Jesus' message is summed up in 1:15: "The kingdom of God is near. Repent and believe the good news!"

***he taught them as one who had authority, not as the teachers of the law*.** The teachers of the Law were men schooled in the interpretation of the Law and were responsible for helping the people in general understand and apply the Law to their situations. Their authority lay in their ability to quote the teachings of previous rabbis on the subject at hand. In contrast, Jesus taught directly. An example is seen in Matthew's version of the Sermon on the Mount in which Jesus counters traditional teaching with his repeated statement, "But I tell you ..." (Matt. 5:22,28,32,34,39,44) without the use of quotes from earlier rabbis to back him up. Jesus didn't need to quote human authorities because his authority was directly from God.

1:23 *an evil spirit.* The Gospels frequently refer to these malignant, supernatural beings, able to harm and even possess people. We are not told what manifestation this spirit exhibited in this man's life, but from other stories in the New Testament we learn that a demonic spirit's activity can range from giving people a supernatural ability to foresee the future (Acts 16:16) to leading people to destructive, violent behaviors (Mark 5:1–5; 9:17). The reality of evil spirits was widely acknowledged in the ancient world (as well as in most parts of the world today that have not become closed to the reality of the supernatural). The biblical understanding is that such spirits were Satan's legions who joined with him in the ancient revolt against God. While not all sickness or bizarre behavior was attributed to the work of evil spirits, such ailments were thought to be common manifestations of possession by a spirit. Given their prominence in the Gospels in contrast to their relative absence elsewhere in the Bible, it seems that their activity is especially exposed in the light of the presence of Jesus. In overcoming this evil spirit, Jesus demonstrated his power over Satan. He has come to bind the strong man (Mark 3:27), freeing people for God. The kingdom of God will be marked by the absence of such destructive forces. This is the start of an ongoing battle.

1:24 *What do you want with us, Jesus of Nazareth?* At first the evil spirit is defiant and resistant.

I know who you are. By identifying Jesus, first using his human name and then by his divine title, the demon was relying on ancient magical practices in the hope of gaining mastery over Jesus. It was believed that knowledge of a person's true identity (or secret name) gave one power over that person. Since the demon named Jesus, supposedly he would have Jesus in his power. However, such a tactic did not work with Jesus!

the Holy One of God. The evil spirit recognizes Jesus for who he is—the divine Son of God. In contrast, it will be quite some time before anyone else, including the disciples, understands this.

1:25 *Be quiet!* Far from being overcome by the demon's ability to name him, Jesus orders the demon to be silent. This is yet another way in which Jesus asserts his authority over the demon. Throughout the Gospels, Jesus does not allow the demons to bear witness to him.

sternly. Literally, this is "he rebuked him." The same word is used in Mark 4:39 when Jesus orders the tumult of the sea and wind to be still. The intent of the word is to show Jesus as the one who has authority to control and restrain the forces leading to chaos.

Come out of him! In Jesus' day there were exorcists who used a combination of religious and magical practices to try to release people whose personality had been invaded and warped by an evil spirit. It was an elaborate, mysterious process with a questionable success rate. In contrast, Jesus issues a simple word of command which is immediately obeyed.

1:26 *came out of him.* Where did the spirit go? According to Jude 6, Christ's judgment upon such spirits is to bind them until the Day of Judgment at which time they will experience the judgment of hell. In spite of popular thought, hell is not the realm where Satan and his demons are in charge: the New Testament pictures it as the place of their everlasting torment.

1:27 Mark notes the two things about Jesus that caught the attention of the people: the quality of his teaching and the power of his actions.

amazed. See note on verse 22. The amazement here is not over the presence of the man with a demon in their midst, since that would not have been an unexpected phenomenon for people aware of and open to spiritual reality. What amazed them was Jesus' power over the demon. Such amazement contains not only joy but some alarm and even fear. Who is this man who possesses such unsuspected power?

1:28 *News about him spread.* The people had witnessed amazing power and heard extraordinary teaching and so it is not at all surprising that they told everyone they met what had happened in the synagogue. Jesus' power over the spirits led him to become a sought-after person in the region (see Mark 1:32; 2:1–2; 3:7–10).

UNIT 3— A Man With Leprosy / Mark 1:40–45

A Man With Leprosy

⁴⁰*A man with leprosy came to him and begged him on his knees, "If you are willing, you can make me clean."*

⁴¹*Filled with compassion, Jesus reached out his hand and touched the man. "I am willing," he said. "Be clean!" ⁴²Immediately the leprosy left him and he was cured.*

⁴³*Jesus sent him away at once with a strong warning: ⁴⁴"See that you don't tell this to anyone. But go, show yourself to the priest and offer the sacrifices that Moses commanded for your cleansing, as a testimony to them." ⁴⁵Instead he went out and began to talk freely, spreading the news. As a result, Jesus could no longer enter a town openly but stayed outside in lonely places. Yet the people still came to him from everywhere.*

READ

First Reading / First Impressions: What is your initial impression about Jesus as you read this story?

Second Reading / Big Idea: Given all the stories about Jesus he could have told (see John 20:30), why might Mark have decided this one definitely needed to be included?

SEARCH

1. Reading between the lines, what do you think the leper was feeling as he approached Jesus (v. 40; see notes)?

2. Given that no one ever touched a leper, what is significant about Jesus' touch prior to his words of healing (see notes on v. 41)? What effect do you suppose this touch had on the leper?

3. The early church used these stories as illustrations of how Jesus frees people from sin. What parallels between leprosy and sin come to your mind as you consider their effect in the life of a person?

4. Put yourself in the place of the disciples watching Jesus during this scene. What insights do you gain about him by observing him here?

5. How do you account for Jesus' commands to the man in verse 44 (see notes)?

APPLY

1. During times when you have felt like a leper, despising your very self and sure that you were cut off from God, how would you describe what Christ did for you then?
   ❒ He touched me through my personal times of prayer.
   ❒ He touched me through the compassion of someone else.
   ❒ He touched me through a change in my circumstances.
   ❒ He touched me through a sense of inner peace even though nothing changed.
   ❒ He touched me through the way my church responded to my need.
   ❒ I'm still waiting for his touch.
   ❒ other:_____

2. The call to silence was a temporary measure for a particular purpose. Typically, the Scripture calls us to tell others of God's good work in our lives. What is one thing God has done for you for which you are especially grateful? Who could you encourage by sharing this news? How could you do so?

3. Jesus risked both his health and his reputation by touching this man. What groups of people have you taken a risk in reaching out to? How has God met you as you took that risk? What risks are before you now in terms of reaching out to others?

GROUP AGENDA

Every group meeting has three parts: (1) To Begin (10–15 minutes) to break the ice; (2) To Go Deeper (30 minutes) for Bible Study; and (3) To Close (15–30 minutes) for caring and prayer. When you get to the second part, have someone read the Scripture out loud and then divide into groups of 4 (4 at the dining table, 4 at the kitchen table, etc.). Then have everyone come back together for the third part.

TO BEGIN / 10–15 Min. (Choose 1 or 2)

1. Have you ever been quarantined at home because you had an infectious condition?

2. Who do you remember having the most compassion for you when you got hurt or sick?

3. Who are the social outcasts and "lepers" in our society?

TO GO DEEPER / 30 Min. (Choose 2 or 3)

1. If you have done the homework, what stands out to you the most from the READ and SEARCH questions or the study notes?

2. What was the leper really saying in his statement to Jesus, "If you are willing, you can make me clean"?

3. When the leper was cured and "cleansed," what difference would this make in his everyday life?

4. What is the closest you have come to experiencing a miraculous healing personally?

5. CASE STUDY: Your friend Bill has only been a Christian for a short time. He just found out he has a sexually transmitted disease, which he contracted before coming to Christ and changing his lifestyle. He feels so guilty about his past that he is having a hard time even praying about his situation, let alone asking for God's physical healing. "After the way I've lived, why would Jesus be willing to do anything about this?" How could you use this story to help Bill?

TO CLOSE / 15–30 Min.

1. Has your group started on the six steps toward fulfilling your mission—from the center section?

2. Share your answer to one or more of the questions in APPLY.

3. How do you need Jesus' "special touch" right now? How can the group support you in prayer?

NOTES

Summary. Mark ends the first chapter of his Gospel with an account of a powerful healing. This is the first of three stories in Mark that lead up to Jesus' declaration of his mission as having come as a doctor "not for the healthy ... but the sick" (2:17). In this story, Jesus deals with a man with an obvious physical problem. Leprosy serves as a particularly apt illustration of sin and evil. Like sin, it brings progressive physical and psychological disintegration, it disfigures both body and soul, it alienates people from one another, it leads those it infects to despise their own selves, and it cuts people off from the worship of God (since lepers were forbidden from coming to the temple). Perhaps most tragically, like sin it was beyond one's ability to change. This miracle implies that in the presence of Jesus, sin, like this man's leprosy, no longer has the final word about a person's destiny.

1:40 *leprosy.* No disease was dreaded more than leprosy since it brought not only physical disfigurement but, because of fear of contamination, social banishment as well. At this time, leprosy was a word used to describe not only the true leprosy known today as Hansen's disease, but was applied to a wide range of serious skin diseases. While the Old Testament Law called for the banishment of lepers, in Jesus' day lepers were prohibited only from living in Jerusalem and a few other ancient cities. Although lepers could live where they wanted, they were considered religiously unclean. Thus, the rabbis developed elaborate regulations regarding how they were to be avoided in order to maintain one's ritual purity. This underlined their social isolation and sense of self-hatred.

came to him. What the leper did was forbidden by law. The leper should have sought to avoid drawing near Jesus so as not to render him religiously unclean. The rabbis taught that if a leper passed by a clean man, the clean man would not become unclean. However, if the leper stopped, then the clean man would become unclean.

If you are willing, you can make me clean. Whether through actually seeing Jesus perform healings (Mark 1:32–34) or through hearing reports of his ability, the leper has a strong faith in Jesus' power to heal. His only concern is whether Jesus would be willing to do so or not, probably a reflection on the leper's terribly crushed self-esteem.

1:41 *Filled with compassion.* Human suffering evoked a deep, affective response from Jesus. He was not afraid of strong emotions.

reached out his hand and touched the man.
Actually touching a leper was unimaginable to most first-century people. Not only did one risk contracting the disease, but such contact made the healthy person ritually impure and thus unable to participate in the religious life of the community. By this gesture, Jesus showed his lack of concern for the details of religious tradition when they came into conflict with human need. From the leper's perspective, the effect of Jesus' touch must have been overwhelming. He had undoubtedly come to think of himself as untouchable and unlovable. This touch affirmed him as a person of worth, in spite of his disease.

1:42 Immediately. This is a favorite word for Mark. In this context it shows the immediacy and efficacy of Jesus' word. It is reminiscent of the word of God in creation as seen in Genesis 1 in which "And God said ..." is immediately followed by "And it was so."

1:43 Jesus sent him away at once with a strong warning. The NRSV has "after sternly warning him," which better captures the note of harshness and rebuke implied in the word used here. While the parallel stories in Luke and Matthew report how Jesus ordered him not to tell others, they lack the strength of the term Mark uses here. It may be that this reflects more closely an eyewitness account of the event. The stern charge may have been to prevent what did indeed end up happening. The man did tell others, resulting in Jesus' inability to continue his preaching ministry as he had intended.

at once. This is the same word translated in verse 42 as "immediately." It emphasizes Jesus' decisive, urgent action.

1:44 don't tell this to anyone. Throughout the Gospels, Jesus repeatedly urges those who have experienced a private miracle not to tell others, the one exception being the demoniac in Mark 5:19. That exception to the rule offers the insight to explain the call to silence. The demoniac was a Gentile in a Gentile environment. In that context, where there were no messianic expectations, the word could be freely spread that God was doing something even for Gentiles in and through this Jewish man. While that might arouse interest, it would not fuel the political fires that news of the Messiah would (and did) fuel in Israel. John 6:15 shows how quickly the political hopes of Israel for deliverance from Rome could be stirred up. While this was the popular expectation of the Messiah, it was not an expectation Jesus intended to fulfill.

Jesus was the Messiah but not the kind of Messiah that was expected. He needed time to communicate what kind of Messiah he was (he came to die not to conquer by force). Eventually the time for secrecy will be over, but at this early point in his ministry he did not want to rouse false hopes that would make his true mission difficult. He did not want his mission to be sidetracked by those who only sought him out for physical healings, nor by those who would look to him for political advantage.

offer the sacrifices that Moses commanded. In Leviticus 14:1–32 the ritual is outlined whereby a leper is declared "clean." Such certification was vital to a leper: It was that person's way back into human society. This also shows Jesus' respect for the Law.

as a testimony to them. This refers to the priests. Since they were the ones who had to verify a person's cleansing, they would have made an official pronouncement of his healing. Thus, the healing would have been a testimony in two senses. Positively, it would be clear evidence that God was indeed at work in and through Jesus. The rabbis considered curing leprosy as difficult as raising someone from the dead (in the Old Testament, only Moses and Elisha ever successfully cured someone of leprosy). If the priests acknowledged that Jesus had indeed cured this man's leprosy, it would have been a powerful evidence to them of his divine authority. Negatively, if the priests refused to acknowledge Jesus' authority even after validating this remarkable healing, then the healing would be a witness against them in the Day of Judgment since they had seen irrefutable evidence of God's work through him yet still resisted his teaching.

1:45 talk freely, spreading the news. Jesus' command was ignored. The leper's joy could not be contained as he told everyone how he came to be healed. The terms used here are common words used later on in the New Testament to describe the nature and content of Christian preaching. While the man was not to have done so at this time, he does serve as an example of a Christian witness who proclaims the Good News of Christ to all.

Jesus could no longer enter a town openly. His teaching ministry (Mark 1:38) was hindered by the clamor of people coming to him only for exorcisms and healings. While they were a sign of what he had come to do, his real mission was to pronounce the deliverance from sin for those who would repent and seek after God's kingdom (Mark 1:15; 2:17).

UNIT 4—Jesus Heals a Paralytic / Mark 2:1–12

Jesus Heals a Paralytic

2 *A few days later, when Jesus again entered Capernaum, the people heard that he had come home. ²So many gathered that there was no room left, not even outside the door, and he preached the word to them. ³Some men came, bringing to him a paralytic, carried by four of them. ⁴Since they could not get him to Jesus because of the crowd, they made an opening in the roof above Jesus and, after digging through it, lowered the mat the paralyzed man was lying on. ⁵When Jesus saw their faith, he said to the paralytic, "Son, your sins are forgiven."*

⁶Now some teachers of the law were sitting there, thinking to themselves, ⁷"Why does this fellow talk like that? He's blaspheming! Who can forgive sins but God alone?"

⁸Immediately Jesus knew in his spirit that this was what they were thinking in their hearts, and he said to them, "Why are you thinking these things? ⁹Which is easier: to say to the paralytic, 'Your sins are forgiven,' or to say, 'Get up, take your mat and walk'? ¹⁰But that you may know that the Son of Man has authority on earth to forgive sins ...." He said to the paralytic, ¹¹"I tell you, get up, take your mat and go home." ¹²He got up, took his mat and walked out in full view of them all. This amazed everyone and they praised God, saying, "We have never seen anything like this!"

READ

First Reading / First Impressions: If something like this happened on Sunday in your church, what would people say?

❏ "Let's not get carried away."   ❏ "We're for anything that is going to help someone."

❏ "Who is going to pay for the roof?!"   ❏ other:_____

Second Reading / Big Idea: What stands out to you as the punch line of this story?

SEARCH

1. What do you think was going on in the minds of the following persons as the events of verses 1–4 unfolded?

The paralytic:

His four friends:

The owner of the house:

Jesus:

2. The man obviously was brought for healing. Why did Jesus first bring up the whole issue of sin and forgiveness (v. 5; see second note on v. 5)?

3. If you were a teacher of the Law, how would you justify your reaction in verses 6–7 (see notes)?

4. What did Jesus healing this man prove?

APPLY

1. In the last session, sin was compared to leprosy. In what ways have you experienced sin to be like paralysis?

2. In what way have you experienced Jesus' word that "your sins are forgiven"? What freedom has that word brought to you?

3. If you had friends who took you to Jesus for healing today, what kind of healing would you need (e.g., physical, spiritual, emotional, relational)? What is the greatest obstacle your friends would have to help you overcome?

GROUP AGENDA

After the first part, read the Scripture out loud and divide into groups of 4. Then come back together for the third part.

TO BEGIN / 10–15 Min. (Choose 1 or 2)
1. What does your family do for you when you are sick: Pump you full of vitamins? Feel sorry for you? Ignore you? Drag you out of bed? Dial 911?
2. When was the last time you had to go to the emergency room?
3. If you had a crisis in the middle of the night, what four friends would you call?

TO GO DEEPER / 30 Min. (Choose 2 or 3)
1. Based on the homework and the study notes, what new insights about Jesus and his kingdom do you see highlighted in this story? Do any of the READ or SEARCH questions especially stand out to you?
2. What impresses you about the four friends in this story?
3. What event in your life has brought you nearest to God?
4. What is the closest you have come to having a supportive community who cared for you when you were hurting?
5. What friend would you like to bring to Jesus in some way?
6. CASE STUDY: Sally has been battling migraine headaches for several years. A couple of her Christian friends have commented that she must have unconfessed sin in her life or else a lack of faith. Though Sally knows her friends mean well, she is getting frustrated with these insinuations. But on the other hand, she wonders if they might be true. How do you advise Sally?

TO CLOSE / 15–30 Min.
1. Has your group taken the survey for small groups in your church (see page M15 in the center section)? If so, what will you do as a result?
2. Share your answers in APPLY, particularly to the last question.
3. How comfortable do you feel sharing the needs and struggles in your life with this group?
4. How can your friends in this group pray for you?

NOTES

Summary. This is the second of the three stories Mark uses to lead up to Jesus' declaration that he has come as a doctor "not for the healthy ... but the sick" (see Summary note in Unit 3). Whereas in the story of the leper, Jesus only dealt with the man's physical need, here he deliberately introduces the issue of spiritual need. While everyone waits to see if Jesus can heal the paralytic, he brings up an unexpected discussion about sin and forgiveness. Like leprosy, paralysis also serves as a powerful illustration of sin. Sin deadens one's ability to function normally. It leaves people spiritually incapable of walking in God's ways and unable to respond to God's invitations. People are not naturally healed of its effects.

Since the news about Jesus has spread everywhere (1:28,45), it is not surprising that the religious leaders want to know who he is and what he stands for. This is the first of five stories in which the religious authorities probe his orthodoxy, a probing that ends with their resolve to kill him (3:6).

2:1 *home.* Capernaum served as Jesus' base for his travels in Galilee. Quite possibly this was the home of Peter and Andrew (Mark 1:29,32–33).

2:2 *he preached the word to them.* Although Mark does not record much of Jesus' preaching, he continually points out that announcing the news of the kingdom of God was Jesus' main agenda (1:14–15, 38; 2:13; 3:14; 4:1; 6:2,12,34). The miracles he performed were intended as illustrations and examples of what life in the kingdom which he proclaimed would be like. But the crowds were more attracted to the fact of the miracles than to their meaning!

2:3 *a paralytic.* Luke, the doctor, uses (in Greek) a technically more exact phrase to describe this man's illness (Luke 5:18). From that we understand that he was, apparently, a paraplegic with spinal damage.

2:4 *an opening in the roof.* The roof of a typical Palestinian house was flat (it was often used for sleeping) and was reached by an outside ladder or stairway. It was constructed of earth and brushwood that was packed between wooden beams set about three feet apart. This type of roof was easily opened up (and could easily be repaired). A rather large opening would have been required to lower a man on a mat. While this was going on, with the noise and falling dirt, all attention inside would have been diverted from Jesus' sermon to the ever-growing hole.

mat. The bed of a poor person.

2:5 *saw their faith.* Jesus' act of forgiveness and healing is connected to faith. In this case it is the faith of the paralytic's friends. Their faith was shown in the fact that they brought the paralytic and that they overcame in a very clever, determined way the obstacle which prevented them from bringing their friend to Jesus. Both these acts testify to their deep conviction that Jesus could and would heal the man. The story shows that faith is not simply belief, but an "energetic grasping of the help and power of God" (Fuller). This is the first mention of faith in Mark. From this point on, faith (defined as "confident, believing trust" by Mann) clearly becomes the response Jesus looks for and responds to in those to whom he ministers.

your sins are forgiven. This was not what the crowd expected Jesus to say. They anticipated he would say, "You are healed." Jesus says this to deliberately focus attention on the nature of his mission and identity, both of which had been obscured by the crowd's fixation on the miraculous for its own sake.

2:6 *teachers of the law.* These are the scribes, religious lawyers who interpreted Jewish law. Originally, it was their job to make copies of the Old Testament. Because of their familiarity with Scripture, people consulted them about points of law and hence their role evolved into that of teacher and protector of the Law. Luke's account of this story (Luke 5:17–26) states that the scribes had come from "every village of Galilee and from Judea and Jerusalem," indicating that this was an official delegation sent to investigate the orthodoxy of this unknown, enormously popular teacher. It may have been their presence that led Jesus to introduce the matter of his authority to forgive sin, a claim that was sure to generate heated debate!

2:7 *blaspheming.* Blasphemy is the act of expressing contempt for God or usurping the rights of God. Under Jewish law its penalty is death (Lev. 24:16). The teachers of the Law believed that illness was the direct result of sin (e.g., John 9:2), so that the sick could not recover until their sin had been forgiven by God. They also knew that God alone could offer forgiveness. Hence they are distressed that Jesus has said to the paralytic, "Your sins are forgiven." This was to claim in quite explicit terms that he was divine and this was the vilest blasphemy.

Who can forgive sins but God alone? This is an accurate understanding of the Old Testament Scripture. Since sin, despite whatever social consequences it may entail, is primarily an offense against God and his Law, only God is in the position to offer forgiveness. While the great leaders of the Old Testament, such as Moses, David and the prophets, would pray that God might forgive the sins of the people, none of them ever took upon themselves the authority simply to speak in God's stead like this.

2:8 Jesus knows what they are thinking—whether by their body language, by his knowledge of how they would react, or by his divine insight.

2:9 *Which is easier.* Jesus responds to their question (v. 7) in typical rabbinic fashion: he asks them a question. The answer to his question is obvious. It is far easier to say "Your sins are forgiven" than it is to heal the man right then and there. There is no way to verify whether sins have been forgiven, but it is obvious whether a lame man walks or not.

2:10 *But that you may know ... to forgive sins.* If Jesus is able to heal the paralytic the scribes would have to admit that he had, indeed, forgiven the man's sins since their own theology linked forgiveness and healing. The visible healing would verify the invisible forgiveness. If they were consistent, the teachers of the Law would now have to admit that Jesus was God (or at least a representative of God) because it is they who said, "Who can forgive sins but God alone?" (v. 7).

the Son of Man. This is Mark's first use of this title, which becomes Jesus' favorite self-designation. Its roots go back to Daniel 7:13–14 in which the prophet Daniel sees a vision of one "like a son of man" receiving authority to rule over God's kingdom.

to forgive sins. This sentence communicates the central thrust of Jesus' mission toward which this miracle, and all the miracles, were intended to point: Jesus has the power to forgive sin. This is the essential Gospel message.

2:11 *I tell you.* This focuses attention on the authority of Jesus himself. He does not invoke any other name but his own. It is through his divine power that the man is healed (and, by extension, forgiven of sin).

2:12 *This amazed everyone.* Mark's miracle stories usually end with an observation of the amazement of those who witnessed them. The "everyone" would not seem to include the teachers of the Law, who from this time on became more and more resistant to Jesus.

UNIT 5—Jesus Feeds the Five Thousand / Mark 6:30-44

Jesus Feeds the Five Thousand

³⁰The apostles gathered around Jesus and reported to him all they had done and taught. ³¹Then, because so many people were coming and going that they did not even have a chance to eat, he said to them, "Come with me by yourselves to a quiet place and get some rest."

³²So they went away by themselves in a boat to a solitary place. ³³But many who saw them leaving recognized them and ran on foot from all the towns and got there ahead of them. ³⁴When Jesus landed and saw a large crowd, he had compassion on them, because they were like sheep without a shepherd. So he began teaching them many things.

³⁵By this time it was late in the day, so his disciples came to him. "This is a remote place," they said, "and it's already very late. ³⁶Send the people away so they can go to the surrounding countryside and villages and buy themselves something to eat."

³⁷But he answered, "You give them something to eat."

They said to him, "That would take eight months of a man's wages! Are we to go and spend that much on bread and give it to them to eat?"

³⁸"How many loaves do you have?" he asked. "Go and see."

When they found out, they said, "Five—and two fish."

³⁹Then Jesus directed them to have all the people sit down in groups on the green grass. ⁴⁰So they sat down in groups of hundreds and fifties. ⁴¹Taking the five loaves and the two fish and looking up to heaven, he gave thanks and broke the loaves. Then he gave them to his disciples to set before the people. He also divided the two fish among them all. ⁴²They all ate and were satisfied, ⁴³and the disciples picked up twelve basketfuls of broken pieces of bread and fish. ⁴⁴The number of the men who had eaten was five thousand.

READ

First Reading / First Impressions: If you had been in this crowd, what reactions would you have toward what happened in this story?

Second Reading / Big Idea: This is one of the rare stories that occurs in all the Gospels. What about it do you think the writers found especially striking?

SEARCH

1. Jesus said, "Come with me by yourselves to a quiet place and get some rest" (v. 31). If you were one of the disciples, how would you feel when you got there and thousands of people were waiting for you?

2. What attitudes and emotions do you sense in the disciples' response to Jesus telling them to feed the crowd (v. 37; see notes)?

3. This story is full of Old Testament allusions (see Num. 27:15–17; Ezek. 34:11–15; Ps. 23:2). What does this Old Testament background indicate about what this event was meant to reveal about Jesus?

4. What connection do you see between this story and the Lord's Supper (see last note on v. 41)?

5. Mark makes no mention of the disciples' reaction to what happened. If you were one of the Twelve, what thoughts would be running through your mind as you went about picking up the leftovers from what seemed to be a terribly scanty meal? What was the lesson to be learned?

APPLY

1. Although they didn't catch it yet, this event was pivotal in leading the disciples to ultimately see Jesus as the divine Messiah. Given your current understanding and experience of Jesus, how would you describe to a friend who you think he is?

2. What are one or two things that have led you to believe what you do about Jesus? How were they important to you?

3. How does this story contribute to or challenge your perception of Jesus?

GROUP AGENDA

After the first part, read the Scripture out loud and divide into groups of 4. Then come back together for the third part.

TO BEGIN / 10–15 Min. (Choose 1 or 2)
1. What do you do to unwind after a busy day?

2. What is the longest you have gone without food?

3. Of all Jesus' miracles, which is your favorite?

TO GO DEEPER / 30 Min. (Choose 2 or 3)
1. What was something new or significant that you learned about this passage from answering the homework questions or reading the notes?

2. How does this story illustrate that God was doing something through Jesus about people being like "sheep without a shepherd" (v. 34)?

3. Briefly share your answers to the questions in APPLY.

4. When do you feel most inadequate and short of resources as you look at the needs around you?

5. How much of your potential are you giving to God right now (e.g., 5%, 50%, 99%)?

6. CASE STUDY: Mark and Allison have been going through hard times financially. Mark has been laid off twice. Allison would rather stay home with their children but feels obligated to work. They heard a minister on TV use the miracle of the feeding of the five thousand as a basis to say it is God's will that all Christians live in material abundance. They were excited about this biblical application, but are wondering if they should get their hopes up for a supernatural provision in their finances. How would you apply this Scripture to Mark and Allison's situation?

TO CLOSE / 15–30 Min.
1. What is a talent or resource you have that God could use to help others?

2. If your group pooled its time and resources, what special project or mission could you accomplish (e.g., starting a new group)? Are you working on your mission as a group?

3. How can the group pray for you?

NOTES

Summary. Mark uses this familiar story to begin another major section (6:30–8:30) in his Gospel. In the first section (1:14–4:34), the disciples (and others) view Jesus as an exceptionally gifted rabbi. In section two (4:35–6:29), Jesus is discovered to be a man of amazing power. Here in section three, he is discovered to be the Messiah (8:27–30). Thus the disciples' understanding of Jesus continues to unfold. In this section there are two parallel cycles of stories. The point is made in both cycles that it will take a miracle from Jesus to heal the hardened hearts of the Twelve so that they come to see who he really is—or at least to understand as much as they can prior to his death and resurrection. Cycle one (6:30–7:37) begins with the feeding of the five thousand and ends with the healing of a deaf and dumb man. Cycle two (8:1–26) begins with the feeding of the four thousand and ends with the healing of a blind man. In both cycles the reader is shown the inability of the disciples to understand what is happening. It is as if they are deaf, dumb and blind.

6:30 Having returned from their mission to preach, cast out demons, and heal in the villages throughout Galilee (Mark 6:7–13), the Twelve report to the Lord what took place in their travels.

apostles. This is the only time this term is used in Mark. Here it is not so much a title as a description of what they have just done. An apostle is "one who is sent" and they have just completed the missionary work the Lord sent them out to do (Mark 6:7).

6:31 ***get some rest.*** It is Jesus who insists on rest even though the opportunity for ministry is great (see also Mark 1:35).

6:32–44 The importance of the feeding of the five thousand is highlighted by the fact that it is the only miracle described in all four Gospels.

6:33 ***ran on foot.*** The crowds are now wise to the disciples' tactic of simply sailing off across the lake and leaving them standing on the shore (see Mark 4:35–36). So they follow on foot. The distances would not have been great since the lake was only eight miles at its widest. As they run around the lake to get to the place where the boats would land, more and more people from the lakeside villages would join with them, swelling their numbers.

6:34 ***sheep without a shepherd.*** Without a shepherd, sheep are hopelessly lost. They have no way to defend themselves and they will probably starve. This was an apt metaphor for the condition of the crowd. They had been abandoned, by and large, by the religious leaders. Their inability to keep the oral law caused them to be considered "unclean" in a religious sense. This phrase itself is taken from the Old Testament and is one of several Old Testament allusions Mark uses to hint to the reader that the miracle is really intended to show that Jesus is God with us, the True Shepherd of Israel.

6:35 The disciples recognize that they have a problem on their hands. How are they going to feed the enormous crowd that has gathered?

a remote place. This is the third reference to a wilderness area (see also vv. 31–32). This is an allusion to Moses who fed the people of Israel in the wilderness. Jesus clearly makes this connection to himself in John 6:26–51.

6:36 *Send the people away.* This is the disciples' solution! "Let the people buy what they need in the nearby towns." This is not a reasonable suggestion if the situation is viewed in ordinary terms, for there are too many people for the supplies available in the local villages.

6:37 *You give them something to eat.* Jesus has quite a different solution in mind! The response of the disciples indicates they had no clue as to how Jesus expected them to do this. Jesus' statement, and the entire scene, is similar to that found in 2 Kings 4:42–44. In that situation Elisha, a great prophet of the Lord, miraculously provided food for 100 people from 20 loaves of bread. If the people saw that as an act authenticating Elisha's commission from God, how much more should they see the miracle Jesus is about to perform as an act confirming his divine authority?

eight months of a man's wages. Once again, as during the storm on the lake (Mark 4:37–38), the disciples do not expect that Jesus will be able to solve the problem in a miraculous way. The only way they can see to feed the crowd is to buy lots of food.

Are we to go and spend. While this may mean that they did have enough money in their common purse to do this but were reluctant to spend it this way, it is more likely that this was a rhetorical question tinged with sarcasm. Elsewhere in Mark's Gospel, the disciples express frustration at what seems to be Jesus' unreasonable behavior (see 4:38; 5:30–31). Their exasperation with Jesus is evident in their two responses to him in this verse.

6:39 *groups on the green grass.* This descriptive touch is loaded with implications. Mark does not typically use descriptive adjectives (e.g., "green") in his writing. The fact that he does so here suggests an allusion to Psalm 23:2, a psalm of David in which God, the shepherd of God's people, leads his flock to "lie down in green pastures." As with verse 34 (see note), Mark is giving another verbal clue to the reader of the divine nature of Jesus.

6:40 The division of people into these groups parallels what Moses did in the wilderness (Ex. 18:21).

6:41 *five loaves.* These were small round cakes made of wheat or barley. What Jesus does here is what Moses did in the wilderness: he feeds the hungry multitudes (compare Ex. 16; Num. 11).

two fish. These were probably smoked or pickled fish that were used as a sauce for the bread.

gave thanks / broke / gave. There are overtones here of the Last Supper (Mark 14:12–26) and the church's practice of Communion (1 Cor. 11:23–24). The words that Jesus uses parallel the words of institution taken from the description of the Last Supper: "Jesus took bread, gave thanks and broke it, and gave it to his disciples, saying, 'Take it; this is my body' " (Mark 14:22). This feeding, like the Lord's Supper, is a foreshadowing of the feeding of all God's people at the messianic banquet.

6:42 *satisfied.* Miraculously, the five loaves and two fish fed everyone not meagerly but abundantly, so that they were filled. As in the scene with Elisha (2 Kings 4:44), there was more than enough to go around, accenting God's lavish generosity.

6:43 *twelve.* In keeping with the metaphoric nature of this story, the 12 baskets represent the 12 tribes of Israel—reinforcing the idea that this scene has prophetic significance as a demonstration that Jesus the Messiah provides nourishment for all God's people.

basketfuls. These were smaller wicker containers carried by all Jews. Each disciple returned with his container full.

broken pieces. The Law required that scraps of a meal be collected.

6:44 *men.* Literally, this is "males." Matthew 14:21 makes it clear there were women and children present as well. The actual number of people fed far exceeded five thousand.

UNIT 6—Jesus Calms the Storm / Mark 4:35-41

Jesus Calms the Storm

³⁵*That day when evening came, he said to his disciples, "Let us go over to the other side."* ³⁶*Leaving the crowd behind, they took him along, just as he was, in the boat. There were also other boats with him.* ³⁷*A furious squall came up, and the waves broke over the boat, so that it was nearly swamped.* ³⁸*Jesus was in the stern, sleeping on a cushion. The disciples woke him and said to him, "Teacher, don't you care if we drown?"*

³⁹*He got up, rebuked the wind and said to the waves, "Quiet! Be still!" Then the wind died down and it was completely calm.*

⁴⁰*He said to his disciples, "Why are you so afraid? Do you still have no faith?"*

⁴¹*They were terrified and asked each other, "Who is this? Even the wind and the waves obey him!"*

READ

First Reading / First Impressions: If you were a reporter assigned to the Lake of Galilee beat, what headline would you give this event?

❏ "Self-Proclaimed Messiah Proves Himself"
❏ "Religious Leader Gives Followers a Scare"
❏ "Prophet Demonstrates Sleeping Disorder"
❏ "Even Nature Obeys Miracle Worker"
❏ other:_____

Second Reading / Big Idea: Why did Jesus allow a storm to come up in the first place?

❏ He didn't—storms are natural.　　❏ He wanted to stretch their faith.
❏ He was asleep at the switch.　　❏ He wanted to show them something new about himself.
❏ He wanted to test them.　　❏ other:_____

SEARCH

1. If you had been one of the disciples when the boat was about to sink, what would you have done?

❏ jumped overboard　　　　❏ taken command
❏ screamed for help　　　　❏ acted like nothing was wrong
❏ started bailing water　　　❏ woke Jesus up

2. Why do you think the disciples awakened Jesus?

3. At the story's end, do you think the disciples were more afraid of the storm or of Jesus (see first note on v. 40)? Why?

Leadership Training Supplement

YOU ARE
HERE

BIRTH	GROWTH	RELEASE
101	201	301

What is the game plan for your group in the 301 stage?

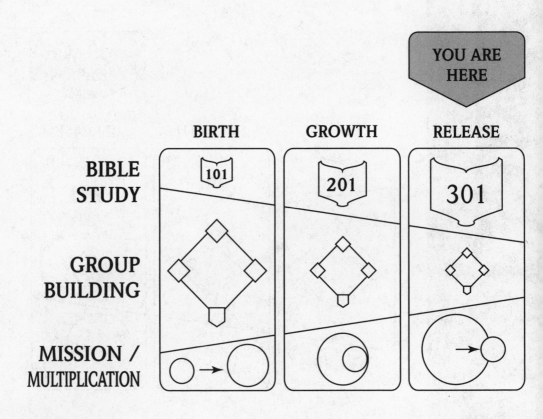

YOU ARE HERE

	BIRTH	GROWTH	RELEASE
BIBLE STUDY	101	201	301
GROUP BUILDING			
MISSION / MULTIPLICATION			

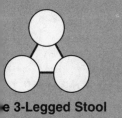

e 3-Legged Stool

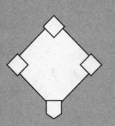

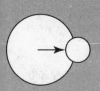

The three essentials in a healthy small group are Bible Study, Group Building, and Mission / Multiplication. You need all three to stay balanced—like a 3-legged stool.
- To focus only on Bible Study will lead to scholasticism.
- To focus only on Group Building will lead to narcissism.
- To focus only on Mission will lead to burnout.

You need a game plan for the life cycle of the group where all of these elements are present in a purpose-driven strategy.

Bible Study

To develop the habit and skills for personal Bible Study.

TWO LEVELS: (1) Personal—on your own, and (2) Group study with your small group. In the personal Bible Study, you will be introduced to skills for reflection, self-inventory, creative writing and journaling.

Group Building

To move into discipleship with group accountability, shared leadership and depth community.

At the close of this course, the group building aspect will reach its goal with a "going-away" party. If there are other groups in the church in this program, the event would be for all groups. Otherwise, the group will have its own closing celebration and commissioning time.

Mission / Multiplication

To commission the members of the leadership team from your group who are going to start a new group.

This Leadership Training Supplement is about your mission project. In six steps, your group will be led through a decision-making process to discover the leadership team within your group to form a new group.

Mission / Multiplication

Where are you in the 3-stage life cycle of your mission?

You can't sit on a one-legged stool—or even a two-legged stool. It takes all three. A Bible Study and Care Group that doesn't have a MISSION will fall.

Birthing Cycle

The mission is to give birth to a new group at the conclusion of this course. In this 301 course, you are supposed to be at stage three. If you are not at stage three, you can still reach the mission goal if you stay focused.

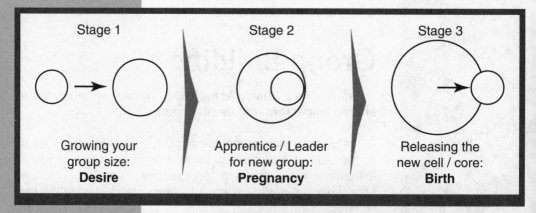

The birthing process begins with DESIRE. If you do not want to birth a new group, it will never happen. Desire keeps the group focused on inviting new people into your group every week— until your group grows to about 10 or 12 people.

The second stage is PREGNANCY. By recognizing the gifts of people in your group, you are able to designate two or three people who will ultimately be the missionaries in your group to form a new group. This is called the "leadership core."

The third stage is BIRTH—which takes place at the end of this course, when the whole group commissions the core or cell to move out and start the new group.

6 Steps to Birth a Group

Step 1

Desire

Is your group purpose-driven about mission?

Take this pop quiz and see how purpose-driven you are. Then, study the "four fallacies" about groups.

Step 2

Assessment

Is your church purpose-driven about groups?

Pinpoint where you are coming from and where most of the people in small groups in your church come from.

Step 3

Survey

Where's the itch for those in your church who are not involved in groups?

Take this churchwide survey to discover the felt needs of those in your church who do not seem to be interested in small groups.

Step 4

Brainstorming

What did you learn about your church from the survey?

Debrief the survey in the previous step to decide how your small group could make a difference in starting a new group.

Step 5

Barnstorming

Who are you going to invite?

Build a prospect list of people you think might be interested in joining a new group.

Step 6

Commissioning

Congratulations. You deserve a party.

Commission the leadership core from your group who are going to be your missionaries to start a new group. Then, for the rest of the "mother group," work on your covenant for starting over ... with a few empty chairs.

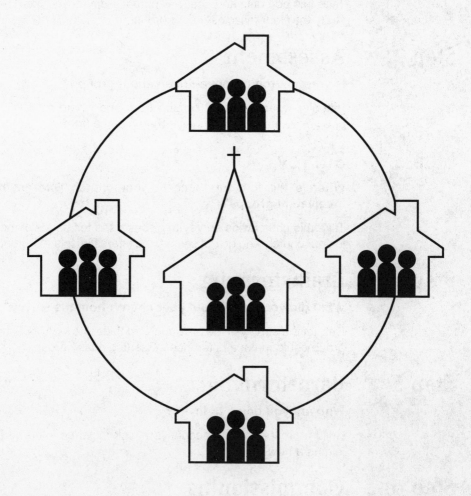

Desire

Is your group purpose-driven about mission?

The greatest danger to any chain is its strongest link. This is especially true of Bible Study groups. The very depth of the study keeps new people from joining, or feeling comfortable when they join. In the end the group grows inward, becoming self-centered and spiritually insensitive.

To prevent this from happening in your group, take this pop quiz and share the results with your group.

	Yes	No
1. Are you a committed follower of Jesus Christ?	❑	❑
2. Do you believe that Jesus Christ wants you to share your faith with others?	❑	❑
3. Do you believe that every Christian needs to belong to a small, caring community where Jesus Christ is affirmed?	❑	❑
4. Do you know of people in your church who are not presently involved in a small group?	❑	❑
5. Do you know friends on the fringe of the church who need to belong to a life-sharing small group?	❑	❑
6. Do you believe that God has a will and plan for your life?	❑	❑
7. Are you willing to be open to what God might do through you in this small group?	❑	❑
8. Are you open to the possibility that God might use you to form a new group?	❑	❑

If you can't say "No" to any of these questions, consider yourself committed!

What Is a Small Group?

A Small Group is an intentional, face-to-face gathering of people in a similar stage of life at a regular time with a common purpose of discovering and growing in a relationship with Jesus Christ.

Small Groups are the disciple-making strategy of Flamingo Road Church. The behaviors of the 12 step strategy are the goals we want to achieve with each individual in small group. These goals are accomplished through a new members class (membership) and continues in a regular on-going small group (maturity, ministry and multiplication).

Keys to an Effective Small Group Ministry

1. Care for all people (members/guests) through organized active Care Groups.
2. Teach the Bible interactively while making life application.
3. Build a Servant Leadership Team.
4. Birth New Groups.

Commitments of all Small Group Leaders are ...

... all the behaviors represented in the 12 step strategy
... to lead their group to be an effective small group as mentioned above.
... use curriculum approved by small group pastor

Taken from the Small Group Training Manual of Flamingo Road Community Church, Fort Lauderdale, FL.

Four Fallacies About Small Groups

Are you suffering from one of these four misconceptions when it comes to small groups? Check yourself on these fallacies.

Fallacy #1: It takes 10 to 12 people to start a small group.

Wrong. The best size to start with is three or four people—which leaves room in the group for growth. Start "small" and pray that God will fill the "empty chair" ... and watch it happen.

Fallacy #2: It takes a lot of skill to lead a small group.

Wrong again. Sticking to the three-part tight agenda makes it possible for nearly anyone to lead a group. For certain support and recovery groups more skills are required, but the typical Bible Study and Care Group can be led by anyone with lots of heart and vision.

Fallacy #3: To assure confidentiality, the "door" should be closed after the first session.

For certain "high risk" groups this is true; but for the average Bible Study and Care Group all you need is the rule that "nothing that is said in the group is discussed outside of the group."

Fallacy #4: The longer the group lasts, the better it gets.

Not necessarily. The bell curve for effective small groups usually peaks in the second year. Unless new life is brought into the group, the group will decline in vitality. It is better to release the group (and become a reunion group) when it is at its peak than to run the risk of burnout.

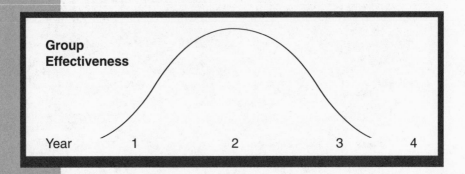

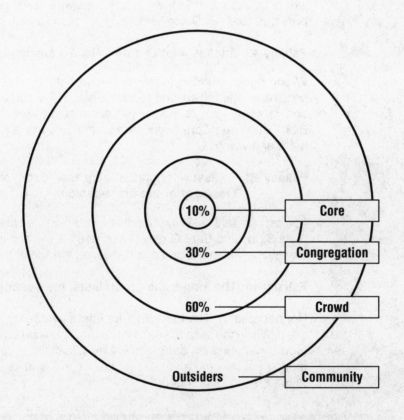

Step 2

Assessment

Is your church purpose-driven about groups?

Most of the people who come to small groups in the church are from the highly committed CORE of the church. How about your group?

Pinpoint Your Group

The graph on the opposite page represents the four types of people typically found in your church and in your community.

- **10% Core:** The "spiritual core" of the church and the church leadership.

- **30% Congregation:** Those who come to church regularly and are faithful in giving.

- **60% Crowd:** Those on the membership roles who attend only twice a year. They have fallen through the cracks.

- **Outside Community:** Those who live in the surrounding area but do not belong to any church.

Step 1: On the opposite page, put a series of dots in the appropriate circles where the members of your group come from.

Step 2: If you know of other small groups in your church, put some more dots on the graph to represent the people in those groups. When you are finished, stop and ask your group this question:

"Why do the groups in our church appeal only to the people who are represented by the dots on this graph?"

Four Kinds of Small Groups

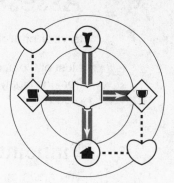

SUPPORT / RECOVERY GROUPS
- Felt needs
- Short-term
- Low-level commitment
- Seeker Bible Study

These groups are designed to appeal to hurting people on the fringe of the church and in the community.

PULPIT-BASED GROUPS
- Around the Scripture in the Sunday lesson
- With handout in Sunday bulletin
- With discussion questions
- No homework

These groups are designed to appeal to those who come to church and listen to the sermon but do not want to do homework.

DISCIPLESHIP / DEPTH BIBLE STUDY GROUPS
- Year-long commitment
- Depth Bible Study
- Homework required
- Curriculum based

These groups are designed to appeal to the 10% highly committed core of the church who are ready for discipleship.

COVENANT GROUPS
- Three-stage life cycle
- Renewal option
- Begins with 7-week contract
- Graded levels of Bible Study: 101, 201 and 301

Church Evaluation

You do NOT have to complete this assessment if you are not in the leadership core of your church, but it would be extremely valuable if your group does have members in the leadership core of your church.

1. Currently, what percentage of your church members are involved in small groups?

2. What kind of small groups are you offering in your church? (Study the four kinds of groups on the opposite page.)
   ❐ Support / Recovery Groups
   ❐ Pulpit-Based Groups
   ❐ Discipleship / Depth Bible Study Groups
   ❐ Three-stage Covenant Groups

3. Which statement below represents the position of your church on small groups?
   ❐ "Small Groups have never been on the drawing board at our church."
   ❐ "We have had small groups, but they fizzled."
   ❐ "Our church leadership has had negative experiences with small groups."
   ❐ "Small groups are the hope for our future."
   ❐ "We have Sunday school; that's plenty."

4. How would you describe the people who usually get involved in small groups?
   ❐ 10% Core   ❐ 30% Congregation   ❐ 60% Crowd

Risk and Supervision
This depends on the risk level of the group—the higher the risk, the higher the supervision. For the typical Bible Study group ⬭ , pulpit-based group ⓨ, or covenant group ◈ (where there is little risk), supervision is minimal. For some support groups ♡ and all recovery groups ⚡, training and supervision are required.

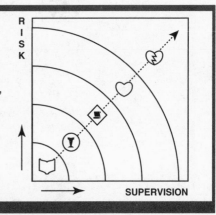

Step 3 Survey

Where's the itch for those in your church who are not involved in groups?

This survey has been written for churchwide use—in hopes that you may be able to rewrite it and use it in your own church. The courses described in this survey are taken from the present Serendipity 101, 201 and 301 courses for small groups.

Churchwide Survey for Small Groups

Name_____Phone_____

Section 1: Interest in Shared-Experience Groups

A shared-experience group is short-term in nature (7–13 weeks) and brings people together based on a common interest, experience or need in their lives. The various topics being considered for shared-experience groups are listed below.

1. Which of these shared-experience courses might be of interest to you? Check all that apply in the grid below under question 1 (Q1).

2. Which of these shared-experience groups would you be interested in hosting or co-leading? Check all that apply in the grid below under question 2 (Q2).

3. Which of these shared-experience groups do you think would be of interest to a friend or relative of yours who is on the fringe of the church? Check all that apply in the grid below under question 3 (Q3).

[101] **VIDEO Electives — 7–13 weeks: Sunday School with Groups**

	Q1	Q2	Q3
1. Dealing With Grief & Loss (Hope in the Midst of Pain)	☐	☐	☐
2. Divorce Recovery (Picking Up the Pieces)	☐	☐	☐
3. Marriage Enrichment (Making a Good Marriage Better)	☐	☐	☐
4. Parenting Adolescents (Easing the Way to Adulthood)	☐	☐	☐
5. Healthy Relationships (Living Within Defined Boundaries)	☐	☐	☐
6. Stress Management (Finding the Balance)	☐	☐	☐
7. 12 Steps (The Path to Wholeness)	☐	☐	☐

Survey The Needs —

101 **BEGINNER Bible Study — 7- to 13-week groups**

	Q1	Q2	Q3
8. Stressed Out (Keeping Your Cool)	☐	☐	☐
9. Core Values (Setting My Moral Compass)	☐	☐	☐
10. Marriage (Seasons of Growth)	☐	☐	☐
11. Jesus (Up Close & Personal)	☐	☐	☐
12. Gifts & Calling (Discovering God's Will)	☐	☐	☐
13. Relationships (Learning to Love)	☐	☐	☐
14. Assessment (Personal Audit)	☐	☐	☐
15. Family (Stages of Parenting)	☐	☐	☐
16. Wholeness (Time for a Checkup)	☐	☐	☐
17. Beliefs (Basic Christianity)	☐	☐	☐

201 **DEEPER Bible Study — Varying Length Courses**

	Q1	Q2	Q3
18. Supernatural: Amazing Stories (Jesus' Miracles) 13 wks.	☐	☐	☐
19. Discipleship: In His Steps (Life of Christ) 13 wks.	☐	☐	☐
20. Wisdom: The Jesus Classics (Jesus' Parables) 13 wks.	☐	☐	☐
21. Challenge: Attitude Adjustment (Sermon on the Mount) 13 wks.	☐	☐	☐
22. Endurance: Running the Race (Philippians) 11 wks.	☐	☐	☐
23. Teamwork: Together in Christ (Ephesians) 12 wks.	☐	☐	☐
24. Integrity: Taking on Tough Issues (1 Corinthians) 12–23 wks.	☐	☐	☐
25. Gospel: Jesus of Nazareth (Gospel of Mark) 13–26 wks.	☐	☐	☐
26. Leadership: Passing the Torch (1 & 2 Timothy) 14 wks.	☐	☐	☐
27. Excellence: Mastering the Basics (Romans) 15–27 wks.	☐	☐	☐
28. Hope: Looking at the End of Time (Revelation) 13–26 wks.	☐	☐	☐
29. Faithfulness: Walking in the Light (1 John) 11 wks.	☐	☐	☐
30. Freedom: Living by Grace (Galatians) 13 wks.	☐	☐	☐
31. Perseverance: Staying the Course (1 Peter) 10 wks.	☐	☐	☐
32. Performance: Faith at Work (James) 12 wks.	☐	☐	☐

301 **DEPTH Bible Study — 13-week groups**

	Q1	Q2	Q3
33. Ephesians (Our Riches in Christ)	☐	☐	☐
34. James (Walking the Talk)	☐	☐	☐
35. Life of Christ (Behold the Man)	☐	☐	☐
36. Miracles (Signs and Wonders)	☐	☐	☐
37. Parables (Virtual Reality)	☐	☐	☐
38. Philippians (Joy Under Stress)	☐	☐	☐
39. Sermon on the Mount (Examining Your Life)	☐	☐	☐
40. 1 John (The Test of Faith)	☐	☐	☐

Section 2: Covenant Groups (Long-term)

A covenant group is longer term (like an extended family), starting with a commitment for 7–13 weeks, with an option of renewing your covenant for the rest of the year. A covenant group can decide to change the topics they study over time. The general themes for the covenant groups that our church is considering are listed on the previous two pages.

4. Which of the following long-term covenant groups would you be interested in?

❐ Singles	❐ Men	❐ Women
❐ Couples	❐ Parents	❐ Downtown
❐ Twenty-Something	❐ Thirty-Something	❐ Empty Nesters
❐ Mixed	❐ Breakfast	❐ Engineers
❐ Young Marrieds	❐ Seniors	❐ Sunday Brunch

Section 3: Pre-Covenant Groups (Short-term)

To give you a taste of a small group, our church is offering a 7-week "trial" program for groups. For this trial program, the group will use the course **Beginnings: A Taste of Serendipity.**

5. Would you be interested in joining a "trial" group?

❐ Yes   ❐ No   ❐ Maybe

6. What would be the most convenient time and place for you to meet?

❐ Weekday morning   ❐ At church
❐ Weekday evening   ❐ In a home
❐ Saturday morning
❐ Sunday after church

7. What kind of group would you prefer?

❐ Men
❐ Women
❐ Singles
❐ Couples
❐ Mixed
❐ Parents
❐ Seniors
❐ Around my age
❐ Doesn't matter

SERENDIPITY

BEGINNINGS

A TASTE OF SERENDIPITY

7 Sessions To Become
A Great Small Group!

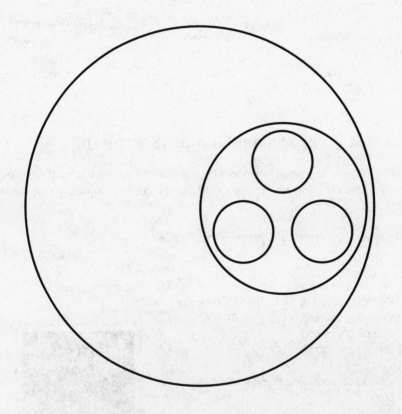

Step 4 Brainstorming

What did you learn about your church from the survey?

The Itch: Debrief together what you discovered from the survey about the need for small groups in your church. To begin with, find out in your group who checked Q3 for any of the 101 Video and 101 Beginner Electives (courses 1–17). Jot down in the box below the top three courses that you checked for 1–17.

Top Three Courses:

The Nitch: For the top three courses in the box above, find out if anyone in your group checked Q2 for these courses—i.e., that they would be willing to host or help lead a group that was interested in this course. Jot down the names of those in your group who checked Q2 in the box below.

Potential Hosts and Leaders:

The Apprentice / Leader and Leadership Core: Now, as a group, look over the names of the potential hosts and leaders you put in the box above and try to discern the person on this list who you think could easily be the leader of this new group, and one or two others who might fill out the Leadership Core for this new group. Jot down these names in the box below.

Apprentice / Leader and Leadership Core:

Q&A

What is the purpose of Covenant Groups?*

The members of the Covenant Group come together for the purpose of helping each other to:

- *Love God with all their heart, soul, mind and strength (Mark 12:30).*
- *Love their neighbors as themselves (Mark 12:31).*
- *Make disciples (Matthew 28:19).*

What are the qualifications of a Covenant Group leader?

A Covenant Group leader functions as a lay pastor, taking on himself or herself the responsibility of providing the primary care for the members of the group. Therefore, a Covenant Group leader exemplifies the following characteristics:

- *believes in Jesus Christ as their Lord and Savior*
- *has been a Christian for a while*
- *continues to grow in their faith*
- *cares for the well-being of others*
- *is able to set goals and work toward them*
- *demonstrates moral integrity*
- *listens to others*
- *is empathetic*
- *is willing to learn from others*
- *demonstrates flexibility*
- *respects others*
- *senses a call to serve*

A Covenant Group leader is not a perfect person! He or she need not know everything about leading and caring for others. Skills valuable to the role of a leader will be taught throughout the year, and care for the leader will be provided on an ongoing basis through a coach.

A Covenant Group leader is not necessarily a teacher. It is far more important that the leader be able to shepherd and care for the others in the group. Teaching is often a shared responsibility among group members.

* These four pages (M20–M23) are taken from the Training Manual For Group Leaders at Zionsville Presbyterian Church, Zionsville, IN, and are used by permission.

Questions & Answers

What does the church expect of a Covenant Group leader?

Every leader is asked to agree to the terms of the leader's covenant. Covenant Group leaders are to attend the monthly STP (Sharing, Training and Prayer) meeting. This gathering is held for the purposes of training and supporting leaders. The meeting takes place on the third Tuesday of each month, from 6:45 p.m. to 8:30 p.m. The two main elements of the STP event concern communication. The first half of the evening is devoted to disseminating the vision. The second half of the meeting consists of leaders huddling with their coach and with each other for the purpose of learning from one another. If a leader is unable to attend this meeting for some significant reason, he or she is to arrange another time to meet with their coach.

Leaders are also to fill out the Group Leader's Summary after every group event. This one-page reporting form takes only 10 minutes or so to complete and is a vital communication link between the staff liaison, the coach and the leader.

What can a Covenant Group leader expect in the way of support from the church?

A Covenant Group leader can expect the session and the staff to hold to the terms laid out in the Church's Covenant.

Every leader will be given a coach. This coach is someone whose ministry is to care for up to five leaders. The coach is charged with the responsibility of resourcing, encouraging, supporting, evaluating, challenging, loving and listening to the leaders in his or her care.

Every coach is supported by a staff member. If leaders ever have a situation where they feel that their coach is unable to help them, the staff liaison is there to be of assistance.

What is the role of a Covenant Group leader?

When people come together in groups, the group itself becomes an entity that is greater than the sum of its parts. The Covenant Group leader watches over the life and health of this new entity.

Leadership Training

Specifically the Covenant Group leader is to:

- *find an apprentice*
- *pray and prepare for group meetings*
- *notify their coach or staff of acute crisis conditions requiring response*
- *develop and maintain an atmosphere in which members of the group can discover and develop God-given spiritual gifts*
- *pray for the spiritual growth and protection of each member*
- *refer counseling cases that exceed experience level*
- *convene the group two to four times each month*
- *recruit a host/hostess, when appropriate, and to see that child care and refreshments are available and a venue is arranged*
- *develop a healthy balance of love, learn, do, decide*
- *assure God's redemptive agenda via Scripture, sharing, prayers, songs and worship*
- *assist the group in refraining from divisiveness or teachings contrary to church position*
- *accept responsibility for group growth through the open-chair strategy*
- *lead an exemplary life*
- *regularly touch base with members outside the context of the group meeting just to say "Hi" and to see how they are doing*
- *help the group form a covenant and to review the covenant periodically*

While the Covenant Group leader takes primary responsibility for these activities, he or she should involve members of the group in many of them.

Does a Covenant Group really have to have a leader?

Yes! Without a leader a Covenant Group is like a ship at sea with no captain. A ship without a captain is at the mercy of the prevailing current and is unable to prepare for what may lie ahead. However, a ship with a captain has her course mapped out, and there is always someone at the helm ready to respond if necessary. So it is with a Covenant Group. The leader serves the others in the group by working to chart the best course as they together pursue being God's people on earth.

What are the critical elements of a Covenant Group?

A Covenant Group needs to have:

- *a leader*
- *an apprentice / leader*
- *members*

- *an open chair*
- *a covenant (see page M32)*

What is an Apprentice / Leader and how do we find one?

An apprentice / leader is someone who agrees that in time he or she will step out into leadership. Historically churches have tended to ask only those who aggressively step forward to serve in leadership positions. Rarely have churches worked at developing leaders. The result has been that most churches experience the phenomenon where only 20% of the congregation does 80% of the work. This historical approach stifles the giftedness of 80% of the church's population! In addition, the church has burned out many of their stand-out leaders by asking them to lead too many programs and too many people. Without some form of apprentice / leadership development, the church is constrained to overload its highly motivated, "here-I-am-send-me" leaders. The apprentice / leader model is meant to address these concerns.

The apprentice / leader is not an assistant. An assistant seldom has plans of stepping into the leader's shoes. Instead, the apprentice / leader works alongside the leader, with the intent of one day becoming a leader themselves. Along the way he or she is experiencing on-the-job training, learning the skills necessary to serve a small group as its leader.

It is the responsibility of the leader to find an apprentice / leader. The most important tools for the leader in this process are prayer and observation. The leader should pray, asking God to send someone whom he or she could mentor and train as a leader. Accompanying these prayers should be efforts to observe those who demonstrate signs of giftedness in shepherding, organizing, listening and faith. The one who is on time and who routinely prepares diligently for the group could be a candidate. The leader could also begin using the time before and after worship services, as well as various fellowship and educational events, to meet others in the congregation. As relationships are established, and the extent of a leader's acquaintances are broadened, the opportunity for finding a suitable apprentice / leader increases.

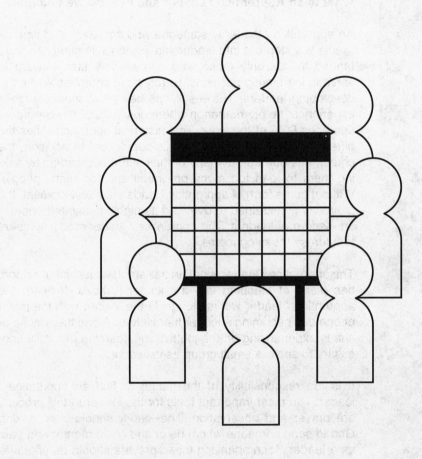

Step 5 Barnstorming

Who are you going to invite?

In the previous step, you identified the Apprentice / Leader and one or two others in your group who are going to be the leadership cell or core to start a new group.

Now, as a whole group, spend a few minutes creating a prospect list of people you would like to invite into this new group. Ask someone in your group to be the secretary and write down in the boxes below the names of people who come to mind:

Friends: Who are your friends in the church who you think might be interested in a small group?

Affinity: What are the special interests of the people in your leadership cell and who are the people in your church with the same interests? For instance, if the people in your leadership cell love tennis, who are the people in your church who might be interested in a small group before tennis? What about book lovers, entrepreneurs, empty nesters, senior citizens, stock watchers, etc.?

How Serendipity 101 Courses
Make Leading A Beginner Group Easy:

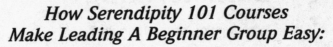

1. *Each session has get acquainted* **Ice-Breakers** *to get your group started and a* **3-Part Tight Agenda** *to keep it on track!*

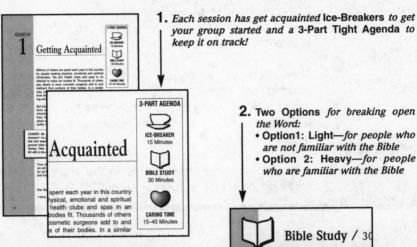

2. **Two Options** *for breaking open the Word:*
- **Option1: Light**—*for people who are not familiar with the Bible*
- **Option 2: Heavy**—*for people who are familiar with the Bible*

3. Study Helps *for the Group Leader include Margin Tips, Reference Notes and Guided Questionnaires for Bible Study.*

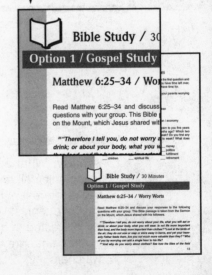

Felt Needs: Who are the people you know with the same felt needs? These people might be on the fringe of the church or even outside of the church. Go back to the survey on pages M15–M16 (the 101 courses) and think of people you feel could be hot prospects. For instance, who would be interested in "Stressed Out," "Marriage," "Wholeness," "Healthy Relationships," "Parenting Adolescents," etc.?

Geographical Location: Where do the people in your leadership team live or work, and who are the people in your church in the same area?

The Four Circles: Now, on this diagram, pinpoint the people you have jotted down in the four circles. Do you have any people on this list from the **Crowd** (the church dropouts)? Do you have anyone on your list from the **Community** (who do not attend any church)? It's really important that you have people from all four circles on your list.

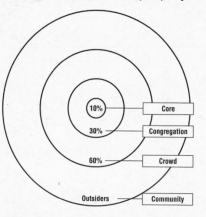

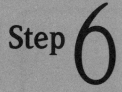

Step 6

Commissioning

Congratulations. You deserve a party.

Only two things remain for you to decide: (1) How are you going to commission the leadership team for the new group and (2) What is the rest of your group going to do next?

Going-away party

You have several options. If the church is planning a church-wide event for all of the groups (such as a graduation banquet), you would have a table at this event for your group. If your church is not planning an event, you must plan your own going-away party.

At this party, you may want to reminisce about your life together as a group with the questions below, have fun making some "Wild Predictions" (see page M30), share a Bible Study time (see page M31), and conclude with a time of commissioning and prayer.

Reminiscing Questions

1. What do you remember about the first time you attended this group?

2. How did you feel about opening up in this group and sharing your story?

3. What was the funniest thing that happened in this group?

4. What was the high point for you in this group?

5. What will you miss most about this group?

6. How would you like this group to stay in touch with each other after you multiply?

7. How did this group contribute to your life?

8. What is the biggest change that has occurred in your life since joining this group?

Wild Predictions

Try to match the people in your group to the crazy forecasts below. (Don't take it too seriously; it's meant to be fun!) Read out loud the first item and ask everyone to call out the name of the person who is most likely to accomplish this feat. Then, read the next item and ask everyone to make a new prediction, etc.

THE PERSON IN OUR GROUP MOST LIKELY TO ...

Make a million selling Beanie Babies over the Internet

Become famous for designing new attire for sumo wrestlers

Replace Vanna White on *Wheel of Fortune*

Appear on *The Tonight Show* to exhibit an acrobatic talent

Move to a desert island

Discover a new use for underarm deodorant

Succeed David Letterman as host of *The Late Show*

Substitute for John Madden as Fox's football color analyst

Appear on the cover of *Muscle & Fitness Magazine*

Become the newest member of the Spice Girls

Work as a bodyguard for Rush Limbaugh at Feminist convention

Write a best-selling novel based on their love life

Be a dance instructor on a cruise ship for wealthy, well-endowed widows

Win the blue ribbon at the state fair for best Rocky Mountain oyster recipe

Land a job as head librarian for Amazon.com

Be the first woman to win the Indianapolis 500

Open the Clouseau Private Detective Agency

Reflection Bible Study

Barnabas and Saul Sent Off — Acts 13:1–3, NIV

13 *In the church at Antioch there were prophets and teachers: Barnabas, Simeon called Niger, Lucius of Cyrene, Manaen (who had been brought up with Herod the tetrarch) and Saul. ²While they were worshiping the Lord and fasting, the Holy Spirit said, "Set apart for me Barnabas and Saul for the work to which I have called them." ³So after they had fasted and prayed, they placed their hands on them and sent them off.*

1. Why do you think God chose this small group in Antioch to launch the first missionary journey (instead of the church headquarters in Jerusalem)?
   ❏ It was merely coincidental.
   ❏ They were following the leading of the Holy Spirit.
   ❏ They were a bunch of outcasts from the fringe of the church.
   ❏ They didn't know how to "paint inside the lines."

2. How do you think the leadership back in Jerusalem felt when they heard what these guys were doing?
   ❏ thrilled   ❏ angry that they didn't follow protocol
   ❏ embarrassed   ❏ They probably didn't hear about it until later.

3. Why do you think the small group chose two people to send out instead of one?
   ❏ for companionship
   ❏ They had different gifts: Paul was a hothead, Barnabas an encourager.
   ❏ It was coincidental.

4. As you think about sending out some members of your small group to give "birth" to a new group, what is your greatest concern for these people?
   ❏ keeping the faith   ❏ keeping their personal walk with Christ
   ❏ keeping the vision   ❏ keeping in touch with us for support

5. As one who is going to lead or colead a new group, how would you describe your emotions right now?
   ❏ a nervous wreck   ❏ delivery room jitters
   ❏ pregnant with excitement   ❏ Ask me next week.

6. If you could say one word of encouragement to those who are going to be new leaders, what would it be?
   ❏ I'll be praying for you.   ❏ You can do it.
   ❏ Call me anytime.   ❏ It's okay to fail.

What do we do next?

For those who are going to stay with the "mother group," you need to decide on your new covenant and who you are going to invite to fill the empty chairs left by the departing "missionaries."

Do we ever meet again?

Definitely! Plan NOW for "homecoming" next year when the new group returns for a time of celebration. Four good times: the World Series, Super Bowl, Final Four and Stanley Cup.

Group Covenant

Any group can benefit from creating or renewing a group covenant. Take some time for those remaining in the "mother group" to discuss the following questions. When everyone in the group has the same expectations for the group, everything runs more smoothly.

1. The purpose of our group is:

2. The goals of our group are:

3. We will meet for _____ weeks, after which we will decide if we wish to continue as a group. If we do decide to continue, we will reconsider this covenant.

4. We will meet _____ (weekly, every other week, monthly).

5. Our meetings will be from _____ o'clock to _____ o'clock, and we will strive to start and end on time.

6. We will meet at _____
or rotate from house to house.

7. We will take care of the following details: ❑ child care   ❑ refreshments

8. We agree to the following rules for our group:

   ❑ PRIORITY: While we are in this group, group meetings have priority.

   ❑ PARTICIPATION: Everyone is given the right to their own opinion and all questions are respected.

   ❑ CONFIDENTIALITY: Anything said in the meeting is not to be repeated outside the meeting.

   ❑ EMPTY CHAIR: The group stays open to new people and invites prospective members to visit the group.

   ❑ SUPPORT: Permission is given to call each other in times of need.

   ❑ ADVICE GIVING: Unsolicited advice is not allowed.

   ❑ MISSION: We will do everything in our power to start a new group.

4. Up to this point, the disciples seemed to assume Jesus was simply a better-than-average rabbi. Look at Psalm 46:10; 65:5–7; 89:9; 107:23–31. What is the significance of these Psalms for interpreting what Jesus was revealing about himself through this event?

5. What question did this story leave the disciples to consider (see second note on v. 41)?

APPLY

1. Reflect on what you have thought about Jesus at different times since you have been exposed to him. Check the categories that have applied at different times in your life:

   ❏ a nice man, like my grandfather   ❏ the founder of a religion
   ❏ a legendary figure, like Santa Claus   ❏ a social revolutionary
   ❏ a miracle worker with special powers   ❏ a spiritual philosopher and teacher
   ❏ God incarnate   ❏ a saint (more spiritual than real)
   ❏ a holy man who commands respect   ❏ a close friend
   ❏ a stern judge   ❏ a prophet
   ❏ the Lord and Savior sent from God   ❏ other:_____
   ❏ an impractical idealist out of touch with the way the world is

2. What insights, experiences or teachings have been especially significant in either leading you to shift from one perspective to another or in confirming your understanding? What are one or two practical differences those insights, etc. have made in how you live?

3. When have you felt like the disciples in verse 38, wondering whether or not Jesus cared about the plight that was overtaking you? What happened? What did you learn through that experience?

GROUP AGENDA

After the first part, read the Scripture out loud and divide into groups of 4. Then come back together for the third part.

TO BEGIN / 10–15 Min. (Choose 1 or 2)
1. When you were a child, where did you go to be safe or to hide when there was a bad storm?

2. What is the closest you have come to experiencing a natural disaster?

3. Who in your family is good at keeping calm in the storms of life?

TO GO DEEPER / 30 Min. (Choose 2 or 3)
1. What stands out to you from this story based on the homework assignment and the study notes? In this miracle, what did Jesus show he had power over?

2. What was the tone in Jesus' voice when he said, "Why are you so afraid?" Was he angry, disappointed, compassionate, or just inquisitive?

3. What was the difference in the fear of the disciples during the storm and their fear at the end of the story?

4. What brings on most of the "storms" in your life? What do you do when they occur?

5. As time goes on, have you seen improvement in the way you handle storms? What difference does your faith in Christ make?

6. CASE STUDY: Your friend Glen comes to you. He's feeling confused: Some Christians claim that believers shouldn't have fears or continuous worries; others say that is a position of denial and that Glen should be honest with his fears and worries and stop having unrealistic expectations of Christianity. Both sides have plenty of Scriptures to back their view. How do you help Glen?

TO CLOSE / 15–30 Min.
1. Are you thinking and dreaming about your group's mission? (See the center section.)

2. Encourage everyone to share—as much as time allows—their responses in APPLY.

3. What stress or worry do you have that you need Jesus to calm? If Jesus were to speak the words to you, "Quiet! Be still!" what would they mean?

4. How can the group pray for you?

34

NOTES

Summary. This story begins a new section in Mark's Gospel. Prior to this passage, both Jesus' enemies and friends regarded Jesus as a rabbi. To be sure, he was not a typical rabbi in that the content and form of his teaching (e.g., 1:27) and his profound ability to heal (e.g., 1:34) and perform exorcisms (e.g., 1:39) differed greatly from the norm. Nevertheless, both friend and foe assumed they understood basically who he was: however accomplished he was at his work, it still fit into the known category of the type of thing a rabbi would do. This story is the first of four miracle stories which explode that category. Through these four stories, a whole new side of Jesus is revealed. While the earlier miracles in Mark dealt with healings and exorcisms which, while certainly notable, were not without parallel among other rabbis, now he demonstrates his authority over the forces of nature and death. These four stories unveil the unique, awesome power of Jesus. The disciples see that he has authority over the very elements of nature (4:35–41); over the most extreme case of possession by evil (5:1–20); over long-term, seemingly incurable disease (5:24–34); and even over death itself (5:21–24,35–43). No rabbi had this kind of power. Through these stories, Mark is showing that Jesus simply does not fit into any of the traditional categories of holy men or respected teachers which the disciples may have had for Jesus: His works indicate he is set far apart from any rabbi or prophet. These stories reopen the whole question regarding the identity of Jesus.

4:35 *That day.* This story is set in the context of Jesus' teaching on the western shore of the Sea of Galilee (see Mark 4:1).

when evening came. The voyage begins as the sun is setting.

4:36 *There were also other boats with him.* Although these boats do not play any other role in the story, their mention, as well as that of other details not found in the parallel accounts (Matt. 8:23–27; Luke 8:22–25), indicate an eyewitness testimony of the event. Presumably the people in these boats were also saved when Jesus stilled the storm.

4:37 *A furious squall.* The Sea of Galilee was a deep, freshwater lake, 13 miles long and eight miles wide at it widest point. It was pear-shaped and ringed by mountains, though open at its north and south ends. Fierce winds blew into this bowl-shaped sea, creating savage and unpredictable storms.

waves broke over the boat, so that it was nearly swamped. In this succinct phrase Mark identifies the problem. The boat was filling with water. This reduced its maneuverability, and eventually would sink it. Bailing the water out of the boat was, therefore, of utmost importance.

4:38 *sleeping.* In the Old Testament, sleeping peacefully is a sign of trust in the power of God (e.g., Ps. 4:8). The fact that Jesus was asleep during a storm is also a sign of his exhaustion from a day of teaching.

on a cushion. This was probably a cushion used for the rowers to sit upon.

Teacher. Up to this point, the disciples understood Jesus to be a rabbi.

don't you care if we drown? This is a rebuke. Jesus' rest in the midst of the storm was not seen as a sign of his trust in God to protect and deliver him, but as a sign of his callousness toward the plight of the disciples. "Other instances of impertinence on the part of the disciples occur in 5:31; 6:37 and 8:4. These instances of rebuke indicate the extent of the veiledness of Jesus' person; the Son of God is subjected to the rudeness of men" (Lane). The disciples were scared. They woke him up simply so he could help them bail out the boat since it was about to be swamped (v. 37). As their later response indicates (v. 41), they had no expectation that he would have any power over the storm.

4:39 Instead of bailing, Jesus commands the wind and the waves to be still ... and they obey. Thus, he demonstrates his power over the very elements in the same way that God does (see Ps. 65:7; 106:9). This was something no ordinary rabbi could do.

Be still! This is literally, "Be muzzled!" as if the storm were some wild beast needing to be subdued. The same word was used to cast out the demon in the story in Mark 1:25. This command to silence presses God's peace into the strife that fights against God and his ways.

completely calm. This was a genuine miracle. When Jesus spoke it was not a matter of the wind beginning to slacken and the waves starting to die down. At one moment the Sea of Galilee was smooth and placid. What Jesus has done here reflects God's power and authority over the sea (see Ps. 65:7; 89:9; 106:9; 107:23–32). Perhaps the most vivid example of God's power over the sea was his parting of the Red Sea so that Israel could pass through.

4:40 *afraid.* Some of the disciples were fishermen who knew how serious their peril was in the face of the storm. Because of the danger, actual fear for their lives was not inappropriate! However, once Jesus displays his power, their fear of the storm turns into fear of Jesus. This is the fear of the unknown and the unexplainable. The disciples were totally unprepared for this action.

Do you still have no faith? Faith here is "faith in God's helping power present and active in Jesus" (Cranfield). Although Jesus had not yet performed any miracle of this nature, the disciples "should by this time have learned something of the secret of the kingdom of God, which is the secret that the kingdom is come in the person and work of Jesus" (Cranfield). This miracle would force the disciples to reconsider all they had heard and seen from Jesus: What had he said or done that should lead them to expect he could act like this?

4:41 *terrified.* Terror replaced fear. This is what is felt in the presence of an unknown force or power. It is the response a vision of a demon, angel, ghost or some other strange, supernatural experience would inspire.

Who is this? This is the key question with which Mark wrestles in his Gospel. The congregation in the synagogue where Jesus performed his first miracle in Mark wondered about this (1:27). The religious leaders asked this question (2:7; 3:22). Now his disciples discover that even they do not understand who he is. Only the readers of the Gospel (1:1), God (1:11), and the demons (1:24) know his true identity. The rest of Mark describes how the disciples, in particular, overcome their culturally conditioned assumptions about who Jesus is and, step-by-step, discover his true nature. "In addition to the miracle's significance as a pointer to the secret of Jesus' person, Mark probably saw in it, and meant his readers to see, a symbolic significance. The parallel between the situation of the disciples on the lake and that of the Church in the midst of persecution would naturally suggest itself. (Very early a ship was a symbol of the Church in Christian art.) In the midst of persecution and all manners of perils, if Jesus be truly with his Church, then, even though his help may not at once be felt, his own must never doubt him, and need have no fear" (Cranfield, *St. Mark*, p. 175).

UNIT 7—Healing of a Demon-Possessed Man / Mark 5:1-20

The Healing of a Demon-possessed Man

5 They went across the lake to the region of the Gerasenes.[a] [2]When Jesus got out of the boat, a man with an evil[b] spirit came from the tombs to meet him. [3]This man lived in the tombs, and no one could bind him any more, not even with a chain. [4]For he had often been chained hand and foot, but he tore the chains apart and broke the irons on his feet. No one was strong enough to subdue him. [5]Night and day among the tombs and in the hills he would cry out and cut himself with stones.

[6]When he saw Jesus from a distance, he ran and fell on his knees in front of him. [7]He shouted at the top of his voice, "What do you want with me, Jesus, Son of the Most High God? Swear to God that you won't torture me!" [8]For Jesus had said to him, "Come out of this man, you evil spirit!"

[9]Then Jesus asked him, "What is your name?"

"My name is Legion," he replied, "for we are many." [10]And he begged Jesus again and again not to send them out of the area.

[11]A large herd of pigs was feeding on the nearby hillside. [12]The demons begged Jesus, "Send us among the pigs; allow us to go into them."

[13]He gave them permission, and the evil spirits came out and went into the pigs. The herd, about two thousand in number, rushed down the steep bank into the lake and were drowned.

[14]Those tending the pigs ran off and reported this in the town and countryside, and the people went out to see what had happened. [15]When they came to Jesus, they saw the man who had been possessed by the legion of demons, sitting there, dressed and in his right mind; and they were afraid. [16]Those who had seen it told the people what had happened to the demon-possessed man—and told about the pigs as well. [17]Then the people began to plead with Jesus to leave their region.

[18]As Jesus was getting into the boat, the man who had been demon-possessed begged to go with him. [19]Jesus did not let him, but said, "Go home to your family and tell them how much the Lord has done for you, and how he has had mercy on you." [20]So the man went away and began to tell in the Decapolis[c] how much Jesus had done for him. And all the people were amazed.

[a]1 Some manuscripts *Gadarenes*; other manuscripts *Gergesenes*
[b]2 Greek *unclean*; also in verses 8 and 13
[c]20 That is, the Ten Cities

READ

First Reading / First Impressions: If you were one of the disciples and saw this man coming toward you, what would you do?

Second Reading / Big Idea: What impresses you the most about the demons in this story?
- ❐ their number
- ❐ their physical power
- ❐ their total control
- ❐ their fear of Jesus
- ❐ their path to destruction
- ❐ other:_____

SEARCH

1. Why do you suppose the disciples aren't mentioned in this story (see notes on v. 2)?

2. What is the literal meaning, as well as the symbolic significance, of the name of the demons (see note on v. 9)?

3. What similarities do you see between this story and the story which precedes it about Jesus calming the sea?

4. Why would the townspeople plead with Jesus to leave (vv. 15–17; see notes)?

APPLY

1. Popular culture often compares demon possession to addiction (e.g., "demon rum ruined the man"). With what particular behavior have you struggled to become free?

2. While not all deliverances are as dramatic as this one, how has coming to Jesus led to greater wholeness in your life?

3. When have you felt that you might prefer the old familiar struggles rather than the new uncertain future Jesus introduces in your life? Why is that?

GROUP AGENDA

After the first part, read the Scripture out loud and divide into groups of 4. Then come back together for the third part.

TO BEGIN / 10–15 Min. (Choose 1 or 2)
1. When have you had a vacation turn into something unpleasant and unexpected?

2. How do you feel about horror movies?

3. What criminal have you suspected might be controlled by an evil spirit?

TO GO DEEPER / 30 Min. (Choose 2 or 3)
1. Quickly go through as many of the READ and SEARCH questions as you can.

2. What does Mark's description of this man tell you about the intentions of evil spirits?

3. How does this story affect your attitudes and beliefs about demons and demon possession?

4. What is the most dramatic transformation you have seen Jesus work in someone's life?

5. Have you ever told your family and closest friends how much the Lord has done for you, like the healed man did at the end of this story? If so, what happened? If not, why? What would you like to tell them?

6. CASE STUDY: Since becoming a Christian about a year ago, Kevin has had a strong desire to share his faith with others and to do something that will really make a difference. He especially feels drawn to those who hang out on the "sleazy strip" of his city. Some people in his church are telling Kevin to go for it; but others are warning him that it isn't safe and that it would even be wrong, because Christians are to "avoid all appearance of evil." After reading this Bible story, Kevin is more convinced than ever that God will protect him and that this is what he is supposed to do. What do you think?

TO CLOSE / 15–30 Min.
1. What were your self-reflections in APPLY?

2. Do you ever long to see miraculous radical changes (like the one in this story) happen in your community and through your church? If you could ask God for a miracle for your community or church, what would it be?

3. What else can the group join you in praying for?

NOTES

Summary. We now examine a second exorcism (see Unit 2). This time Jesus confronts a man who is ravished by not one but thousands of demons. This is the ultimate in possession. Once again Jesus demonstrates his power by casting out this combined force of demons and healing a man whose body and personality had been overwhelmed by their evil possession. This is the second of the four "power" stories by which the disciples come to understand that Jesus is no mere teacher.

5:1 *They went across the lake.* Jesus and his disciples were in a boat on the Sea of Galilee. This incident takes place after Jesus calms the fierce storm that threatened to swamp their boat (Mark 4:35–41). Given the fact that Jesus and the Twelve left the Capernaum side of the lake "when evening came" (Mark 4:35), by the time they arrive at the other side it is probably dark.

the lake. This was the Sea of Galilee, a deep, freshwater lake, 13 miles long and eight miles wide at its widest point. It was pear-shaped and ringed by mountains, though open at its north and south ends. Fierce winds blew into this bowl-shaped sea creating savage and unpredictable storms, one of which Jesus and the Twelve had just experienced.

the region of Gerasenes. The precise location of their landing is not clear. However, it is on the other side of the lake from Capernaum, in Gentile territory, probably near the lower end of the lake.

5:2 *Jesus got out of the boat.* No mention is made of the disciples in this story. Given what they had been through in the storm on the Sea of Galilee (Mark 4:35–41) and the fact that they landed in a Gentile region at night in a graveyard with a nightmare-like figure howling at them, it is not surprising that only Jesus seems to have gotten out of the boat to face this terror.

a man with an evil spirit. There was widespread belief that demons could enter and take control of a person's body, speaking and acting through that person. First-century people lived in dread of demons. Thus they avoided places, like cemeteries, where demons were thought to dwell. The demons were understood to be Satan's legions. In overcoming them, Jesus was demonstrating his power over Satan and his work.

5:3–5 The picture painted of this man was that of a living terror: He was naked, physically he was so powerful he could not be subdued, he was cut up and perhaps bleeding, and he cried out in great distress living there among the tombs.

5:6–9 The naming-ritual begins and the demons try to master Jesus by crying out his true identity (see notes on Mark 1:24 in Unit 2). All the while Jesus is commanding the demons to leave the man (v. 8). Finally Jesus, with his superior power, compels the demons to reveal their name (v. 9).

5:7 *Son of the Most High God.* The disciples asked in the previous story who Jesus is (Mark 4:41) and the demon-filled man, with supernatural insight, here points out his divine nature. Interestingly, this title is how God was often referred to by Gentiles (see Gen. 14:18–24; Dan. 4:17).

Swear to God that you won't torture me! It is not clear what they feared. According to Jewish apocalyptic literature, the torment of demons was to take place at the time of the final judgment. Jesus' presence signals to them the beginning of the end times.

5:9 *Legion.* The name for a company consisting of 6,000 Roman soldiers. The man was occupied not by one but by a huge number of demons. This name also conveys the sense of warfare that is going on between Jesus and Satan. The Roman legions were the first-century world's most fierce fighting force. As such it is an apt name for the kind of overwhelmingly powerful possession by evil that had occurred. Even in this ultimate situation, Jesus demonstrates his power over evil. It cannot stand against him even in its most virulent form.

5:10 Again, it is not clear what they feared. Perhaps they feared being banished to hell. Contrary to popular thought, hell is not the realm where Satan and his demons are in charge. The New Testament pictures it as the place of their torment. According to Jude 6, Christ would bind such disobedient spirits until the Day of Judgment. Nor is it clear that being allowed to enter the pigs—who were quickly drowned—was all that more desirable. The fact that they entered into pigs reveals their unclean, corrupt natures.

5:11 *pigs.* This was a Gentile herd. No Jew would raise pigs since they were considered unclean animals (Lev. 11:1–8). For a Jew to eat or touch a pig meant that he or she was defiled and thus unable to participate in worship until a ceremonial cleansing was performed. This was probably a herd made up of pigs owned by various people in town.

5:13 *rushed down the steep bank.* The stampede of the herd gave evidence that the demons had, indeed, been driven out of the man. Their mad suicidal rush to the sea shows what kind of creatures they are. Their destructive impact on the pigs is in sharp contrast to the peace and healing Jesus brought to the demoniac.

5:14–17 The incident is reported to the townspeople, who arrive in mass and find not only the drowned pigs but the healed demoniac.

5:15 *they were afraid.* It might be expected that they would rejoice that this man who had terrorized them and whom they could no longer restrain was now healed. But instead they are fearful of Jesus, who has the power to overcome the demons and destroy their town herd.

5:17 *the people began to plead with Jesus to leave.* They want no part of one who in their eyes would appear to be a powerful magician—or who regarded a single madman to be worth more than their whole town herd.

5:18–20 The focus shifts from the frightened townfolk to the grateful ex-demoniac. He wants to join Jesus' band but is instead commanded to return home and share his story of God's mercy.

5:19 *tell.* In contrast to what Jesus said to the leper: "See that you don't tell this to anyone," (Mark 1:44, Unit 3), he wants this man to share the story of his healing. The difference is that the leper was Jewish and his story might cause people to think that the Messiah had come before they knew what kind of Messiah Jesus was. Gentiles, however, did not have such messianic expectations. Interestingly, what the ex-demoniac could tell them was limited. He could explain what he was like before he met Jesus, what had happened to him when he encountered Jesus, and what little he knew about Jesus. This first Gentile witness to Jesus had no theological training; he simply had an amazing story to tell by which God's nature would be revealed.

5:20 *Decapolis.* A league of 10 Gentile cities patterned after the Greek way of life. This is the first of several ventures by Jesus into Gentile areas, demonstrating what Mark later points out (Mark 13:10; 14:9), that the Gospel is to be preached to all nations.

UNIT 8—A Sick Woman Touches Jesus / Mark 5:24-34

²⁴*So Jesus went with him.*

A large crowd followed and pressed around him. ²⁵*And a woman was there who had been subject to bleeding for twelve years.* ²⁶*She had suffered a great deal under the care of many doctors and had spent all she had, yet instead of getting better she grew worse.* ²⁷*When she heard about Jesus, she came up behind him in the crowd and touched his cloak,* ²⁸*because she thought, "If I just touch his clothes, I will be healed."* ²⁹*Immediately her bleeding stopped and she felt in her body that she was freed from her suffering.*

³⁰*At once Jesus realized that power had gone out from him. He turned around in the crowd and asked, "Who touched my clothes?"*

³¹*"You see the people crowding against you,"* *his disciples answered, "and yet you can ask, 'Who touched me?' "*

³²*But Jesus kept looking around to see who had done it.* ³³*Then the woman, knowing what had happened to her, came and fell at his feet and, trembling with fear, told him the whole truth.* ³⁴*He said to her, "Daughter, your faith has healed you. Go in peace and be freed from your suffering."*

READ

First Reading / First Impressions: What do you think gave this woman the courage to touch Jesus' clothes?

- ❏ She didn't have anything to lose.
- ❏ She was desperate.
- ❏ She believed she would be healed.
- ❏ She thought she could slip away unnoticed.

Second Reading / Big Idea: How would you sum up in a sentence what seems to you to be the key idea of this passage?

SEARCH

1. From the information about the woman given in verses 25–28, what can you assume about what her life is like?

2. In the scene immediately before this one, Jairus directly asks Jesus to help his daughter. Why might this woman choose not to approach Jesus in the same way (see notes on v. 25)?

3. Put yourself in the woman's place. What thoughts might be racing through your mind as Jesus suddenly stops and asks, "Who touched my clothes?"

4. The woman was already healed. Why was it still important to Jesus that the person who touched him be identified (see note on v. 32)?

5. What insights can you gain from Jesus' response to the woman in verse 34 (see notes)?

6. What similarities do you see between this story and the preceding two miracles (the calming of the sea and the healing of the demoniac)? What point is Mark trying to make by grouping these stories together?

APPLY

This is an exercise in imagination and application. Retell this story from the woman's perspective as she recounts it to her family. What aspect of what has happened is most important to you? Why?

GROUP AGENDA

After the first part, read the Scripture out loud and divide into groups of 4. Then come back together for the third part.

TO BEGIN / 10–15 Min. (Choose 1 or 2)

1. Are you the type who would rather suffer with pain than go to the doctor or dentist?

2. How do you feel when you are crowded into an elevator or subway?

3. What's the closest you have come to having a chronic health problem?

TO GO DEEPER / 30 Min. (Choose 2 or 3)

1. If you have completed the homework, choose one of the READ or SEARCH questions to answer. (It's okay if more than one person chooses the same question.)

2. How do the study notes show that this woman needed much more courage than we might realize to approach Jesus like she did?

3. How did you recount this story in the APPLY exercise?

4. Why was this woman healed when nobody else in the crowd was healed?

5. When do you remember being the most desperate for God's help? How did you "reach out" to Jesus?

6. CASE STUDY: Due to a congenital disease, Susan has been confined to a wheelchair for most of her life. She has two major spiritual and emotional struggles. No one consciously rejects her, but Susan just can't seem to feel accepted in her church. Furthermore, she often deals with the feeling that even God views her as "second class" and incomplete. How could you encourage Susan?

TO CLOSE / 15–30 Min.

1. Has your group assigned three people as a leadership core to start a new small group?

2. What connections have you noticed between your physical, emotional and spiritual health? If your body could talk, what would your body tell you about the stress in your life?

3. How can the group support you in prayer?

NOTES

Summary. This is the third of the four "power" stories Mark uses to emphasize Jesus' absolute and universal authority over all forces that oppress humanity (see Summary note in Unit 6). Just as the Gentile demoniacs would have been considered ceremonially "unclean" by the Jews, so this woman with the interminable menstrual flow would be viewed as an "unclean" person to be avoided by those who wished to maintain their purity before God. In this account we see Jesus deal with a long-standing medical problem that had persisted for years, that had been untreatable by doctors, and which had both physical and social consequences for the woman involved. In it we see anew Jesus' awesome power; we get new insight into the role of faith in healing; and we discover the kind of whole-person healing that Jesus brings that restores not only the body but the psyche and the spirit.

This incident is actually sandwiched between the opening and conclusion of the story of Jairus' daughter (Mark 5:21–24; 35–43). Thus the two stories are interwoven, signifying that they are to be understood in relation to each other. Both deal with females who were second class citizens in the first-century scheme of things; both women are unclean (one due to her menstrual flow and the other because she had died); both are confronted by desperate situations which lead to death; and both women are healed by faith through Jesus' touch. In addition, this story relates to the other three in the section from 4:35–5:43 in that all the stories deal with the threat (or reality) of death, all are situations beyond human control, and all accent Jesus' authority in ways that were totally unexpected.

5:25 *a woman was there.* This story interrupts the account of Jairus' daughter. While on the way to Jairus' home to see his dying daughter, this woman, part of the crowd following after Jesus to see what he could do for Jairus' daughter, approached him in secret. She should not have been there in the crowd. Because of the nature of her illness she was considered "unclean." If people touched her, they too would become "unclean" and be rendered unable to participate in ceremonial worship until they went through a prescribed cleansing ritual.

subject to bleeding. This was probably a steady hemorrhaging from her womb. Not only would this lead to obvious physical and emotional problems, but such bleeding rendered her ritually impure (see Lev. 15:25–33). She was cut off from involvement in the religious life of her people, such as worshiping in the temple, and she would have been prohibited from having sexual relations with her husband. Since many people assumed that chronic problems like this were God's judgment upon a person for their sin, she undoubtedly experienced some measure of condemnation from others as well. As a result she has to seek out Jesus in this surreptitious way.

5:26 When Luke the physician told this story (Luke 8:42–48) he dropped out this verse with its rather scathing condemnation of doctors! Mark's point is not to cast aspersions on the medical practitioners of his day, but to highlight the seriousness of the woman's condition. Like the demoniac in the previous story, this woman was beyond human help. She had exhausted all her resources in the attempt to find help but to no avail.

the care of many doctors. Typical cures would have included such things as carrying the ash of an ostrich egg in a certain cloth or drinking wine mixed with rubber, alum and garden crocuses.

5:28 *If I just touch his clothes, I will be healed.* Jesus' reputation as a healer had obviously preceded him. Yet the woman's perception of Jesus at this point was probably that he was some type of magician who possessed remarkable powers that would be transferred to whatever objects touched him. There is no attempt on her part to establish genuine contact with Jesus: she simply wants to brush up against him so that she can be brought in contact with his power.

5:29 *Immediately.* This is a prominent word throughout Mark's Gospel. It emphasizes the irresistible power inherent in Jesus' person. The same word is translated in verse 30 as "at once." This was a real miracle. Then and there she was healed, and she knew it.

5:30 *power.* This is the creative, healing power of God. The implication is not that Jesus had a limited supply of divine energy that was somewhat drained by this event, but that he was the agent through whom God's power was transmitted to the woman.

Who touched my clothes? Jesus desired a relationship with those he helped. He was not an impersonal power source.

5:31 *You see the people crowding against you ... and yet you can ask, "Who touched me?"* As in Mark 4:38, the disciples fail to understand Jesus or what he is about. They can only see that his stopping to ask what seems to be a foolish question is wasting the limited time they have to get to Jairus' house

before his daughter dies. In the press of the crowd undoubtedly many people were touching him, yet Jesus was aware that a special work had been done for one person and he desired to know who that was.

5:32 *Jesus kept looking around.* Jesus insists that the person who touched him identify herself. At first glance this seems cruel since Jesus forces this woman—who should not have been there in the first place and who had a disease she probably would not have wanted to talk about publicly—to identify herself. However, her healing will not be complete without this since her illness had not only physical but emotional and social consequences. In the same way that he insisted that the leper go through the cleansing ritual and thus be admitted back into society (Mark 1:44), here Jesus makes it publicly known that she has been healed so that she can once again have a normal religious and relational life. In other words, he healed her physically, spiritually and socially.

5:33 *trembling with fear.* Fear is a common element in all these four power stories (Mark 4:40–41; 5:15; 5:36). Not only do the people in the scenes face frightening circumstances, but there is fear before Jesus as well. Everyone is caught off guard by his authority that exceeds all their expectations. This woman may have feared that she had done something wrong; she may have feared that Jesus would shame her in front of everyone; she may have feared that her healing would be revoked.

5:34 *Daughter.* This word changes everything. It stresses that she is indeed a child of God, loved and not under his judgment. It affirms that she is no longer a social outcast, but is in community with the other children of God. It establishes a personal relationship of care between Jesus and her that is in stark contrast to the impersonal, magical notions with which she may have approached him.

your faith has healed you. It was her faith that impelled her to reach out to Jesus—the source of healing power. The word Jesus uses to tell her that she is healed comes from the same root as the words "salvation" and "Savior." Spiritual as well as physical healing is in view here.

Go in peace. Jesus did not mean by this "Be free from worry." This phrase means "Be complete, be whole." Although each of these four incidents portrays an extreme situation in which there is no hope humanly speaking, each ends in peace as the result of the power of Jesus (Mark 4:39; 5:15; 5:34; 5:42).

UNIT 9—Jesus Walks on Water / Matthew 14:22-36

Jesus Walks on the Water

²²*Immediately Jesus made the disciples get into the boat and go on ahead of him to the other side, while he dismissed the crowd.* ²³*After he had dismissed them, he went up on a mountainside by himself to pray. When evening came, he was there alone,* ²⁴*but the boat was already a considerable distance from land, buffeted by the waves because the wind was against it.*

²⁵*During the fourth watch of the night Jesus went out to them, walking on the lake.* ²⁶*When the disciples saw him walking on the lake, they were terrified. "It's a ghost," they said, and cried out in fear.*

²⁷*But Jesus immediately said to them: "Take courage! It is I. Don't be afraid."*

²⁸*"Lord, if it's you," Peter replied, "tell me to come to you on the water."*

²⁹*"Come," he said.*

Then Peter got down out of the boat, walked on the water and came toward Jesus. ³⁰*But when he saw the wind, he was afraid and, beginning to sink, cried out, "Lord, save me!"*

³¹*Immediately Jesus reached out his hand and caught him. "You of little faith," he said, "why did you doubt?"*

³²*And when they climbed into the boat, the wind died down.* ³³*Then those who were in the boat worshiped him, saying, "Truly you are the Son of God."*

³⁴*When they had crossed over, they landed at Gennesaret.* ³⁵*And when the men of that place recognized Jesus, they sent word to all the surrounding country. People brought all their sick to him* ³⁶*and begged him to let the sick just touch the edge of his cloak, and all who touched him were healed.*

READ

First Reading / First Impressions: If you had been one of the disciples and saw a figure walking toward you on the water, what would you have said?

☐ "I'm seeing things!"   ☐ "Get me out of here!"

☐ "Do you see what I see?!"   ☐ "I think I ate too many anchovies!"

☐ "Where's Jesus?!"   ☐ I would have been speechless.

☐ "It must be Jesus!"   ☐ other:_____

Second Reading / Big Idea: Complete this sentence: "If I didn't know much about Jesus, this story would lead me to believe that he:_____."

SEARCH

1. This event occurred just after the feeding of the five thousand. In the midst of his growing popularity, why would Jesus choose to dismiss the crowd and go pray by himself (vv. 22–23; see notes)?

2. What light do the following Old Testament Scriptures shed on the meaning of Jesus' miracle and his words here?

"It is I" (literally, "I am") (Ex. 3:14)

walking on the water (Job 9:8; Ps. 77:19)

"Don't be afraid" (Isa. 41:10; 43:2,5)

3. What does Peter's request to walk on the water (and his calling out to him when he was afraid he couldn't make it after all) show about his perception of Jesus?

4. How does Peter's faltering provide an example to every disciple of Jesus Christ (v. 30; see notes)?

5. Taken in combination with the miraculous feeding, how might this experience lead the disciples to the recognition that Jesus is the Son of God?

APPLY

1. When it comes to taking risks, how would you describe yourself?
   ❏ impulsive—quick to step out   ❏ cautious—testing the water first
   ❏ apprehensive—scared to death   ❏ other:_____
   ❏ procrastinating—putting it off

2. When have you, like Peter, taken a risk based on your faith in Jesus? How does Peter's experience contribute to your understanding of what happened with you?

3. Where do you feel God is inviting you to "get out of the boat" now?
   ❏ in my relationships—dealing with a problem
   ❏ in my future planning—doing something I've been afraid to try
   ❏ in my inner life—facing a hang-up
   ❏ in my spiritual walk—putting God first
   ❏ other:_____

GROUP AGENDA

After the first part, read the Scripture out loud and divide into groups of 4. Then come back together for the third part.

TO BEGIN / 10–15 Min. (Choose 1 or 2)

1. What is your most memorable boating experience?

2. When you were growing up, who was the daredevil among your friends?

3. Of all your adventures in life, which was the most daring?

TO GO DEEPER / 30 Min. (Choose 2 or 3)

1. As a result of doing the homework assignment, what stands out to you about Jesus in this story? What stands out to you about Peter?

2. How hard is it for you to believe that Jesus walked on water? How hard is it for you to believe that Peter walked on water?

3. What made Peter sink? How does Peter remind you of yourself?

4. What dreams do you have for the future? What risks are involved?

5. CASE STUDY: Frank and Peggy are concerned about their son Jim, who recently announced his plans to leave his medical practice and prepare for the ministry. Jim hasn't been a physician very long, so he still has lots of debts from medical school—plus a wife and three young children to provide for. Jim says he's "stepping out in faith"—but his parents are afraid he's jumping off a cliff. What do you say to Frank and Peggy?

TO CLOSE / 15–30 Min.

1. Are you satisfied with your group's progress on "stepping out" to develop a mission?

2. Share as much as you have time for from the APPLY section.

3. In what situation in your life do you need to hear Jesus' words, "Take courage! It is I. Don't be afraid"?

4. How can the group pray for you?

NOTES

Summary. Matthew, Mark and John all follow the story of the feeding of the five thousand with this scene (Luke omits it). The accounts differ in some details (Mark and John omit the scene of Peter attempting to walk on the water) and in their emphasis. In Matthew's account there are several miracles reported, not just one. First, the story we are examining comes immediately on the heels of the amazing miracle in which Jesus fed five thousand people with a few loaves and some fish. Second, there is the miracle of Jesus walking on water (Matt. 14:25). Third, there is the miracle of Peter walking on water—which, if anything, is even more amazing. We have already seen Jesus' power over nature, so his walking on water, while extraordinary, fits in with what we have come to expect about him. But to extend this ability to another person is truly awesome (Matt. 14:29). Finally, there is the miracle of healing in which it is only necessary to touch the hem of Jesus' garment (Matt. 14:35–36).

14:22 *he dismissed the crowd.* While neither Matthew nor Mark accounts for the abrupt departure of Jesus from the crowd, the reason is given in John 6:14–15. Apparently the crowd, sensing that the feeding of the five thousand was a sign that Jesus was indeed the messianic prophet for whom they had long been waiting, tried in its enthusiasm to make Jesus their king who would lead them in opposition to Rome. The disciples are sent away, perhaps, to keep them from harm in the face of this zealous crowd, or perhaps to keep them from catching this false messianic fever.

14:23 *he went ... to pray.* In the midst of great success and popular acclaim, once again Jesus goes off to pray. He is quick to acknowledge his dependence on God as the source of his power.

14:24 *the wind was against it.* Once again, as in their slow trip across the lake earlier (Mark 4:37), the elements work against the disciples. This time the problem is not a storm, but a strong headwind that would make rowing very difficult.

14:25 *the fourth watch.* This was the way Roman soldiers marked time. The fourth watch ran from 3 to 6 a.m. Assuming the disciples set out to sea in the late afternoon, they had been struggling at the oars for probably seven or more hours.

walking on the lake. While it has already been established that Jesus is Lord over the wind and the water (Mark 4:39,41), this is another new action that was well beyond the expectations of the disciples.

14:26 terrified. Once before on this lake they were terrified by an event they did not expect and did not understand, namely the calming of the sea by Jesus (Mark 4:41). This is the terror of experiencing something that defies all categories of understanding.

a ghost. The sea, especially at night, was thought to be a dwelling place for demons. The disciples had no idea of what horror might await them as this apparition approached.

14:27 Take courage! It is I. Don't be afraid. This is the language of God. The call to have courage because of God's presence with his people is a common theme in the Old Testament prophets (Isa. 41:10; 43:5; Jer. 1:8).

It is I. Literally "I am." This phrase can just be a simple declaration by Jesus that there is no ghost to be afraid of. However, in the Old Testament this is a phrase used by God to describe himself (e.g., see Ex. 3:1–14 where God reveals himself by this name to Moses in the burning bush). This is the same phrase used by Jesus in his debate with the Jews by which he claims deity (see John 8:58). In the context of Jesus' ongoing self-revelation of himself to the disciples, this is a telling phrase. Jesus is not just a new Moses or another king in the line of David. He is also the Son of God. Since the Old Testament often refers to God as the one who treads on the water (see Job 9:8; 38:16; Ps. 77:19; Isa. 43:2,16), it is clear that his walking on the water was not simply another miracle: like the feeding of the five thousand, this was intended to be a sign of his divine identity.

14:28–32 This scene is found only in Matthew. "The scene of Peter walking (on) the sea contains something entirely unique: It shows the greatness of the promise made to faith within discipleship (14:28–29), but does not remain silent about the inability of the disciple to hold firmly to this promise during a time of testing (v. 30) ... It is probable that Peter is taken as a representative of the disciples (both those with Jesus and those in the church to whom Matthew was writing) in his enthusiastic love and insufficient faith" (Hill).

14:28 Lord, if it's you. "If" should be understood in terms of "since." It is because Peter is sure that it is Jesus on the water that he asks permission to join him. He realizes he can only do so on the basis of Jesus' word and authority. Peter's action demonstrates what faith is all about: it is acting with confidence in Jesus even when circumstances seem to be impossible. It is not a foolhardiness based on personal bravado, but trust in the character of Jesus to protect and guide his people.

14:30 At first it appears Peter was successful in this incredible act. However, the frightening uncertainty of the situation coupled with the power of the wind and waves beating against him led him to doubt Jesus' word; thus, he faltered.

Lord, save me! Peter's cry sums up the cry of all those who find themselves in desperate situations: his hope is solely in Jesus to rescue him from the danger of the sea. Likewise, all disciples are to call upon Jesus to rescue them from the danger of sin. Matthew's story would encourage those in the church who likewise found themselves faltering along the path of discipleship when faced with threats to their safety. Faltering did not in itself disqualify one from Christ's care, instead, it can become a time to reach out afresh to him as Peter did.

14:31 You of little faith. The problem Peter faced was not the circumstances, but inadequate trust in Jesus despite the circumstances. He has not yet fully come to trust in the power and the person of Jesus.

14:33 Truly you are the Son of God. In reality the disciples do not actually grasp who Jesus is until Caesarea Philippi (Matt. 16:16). Their cry here, in the face of the dual miracle of Jesus and Peter walking on water, "represents more the instinctive reaction to a display of supernatural power. As the disciples groped for adequate words to express their awareness that Jesus was more than an ordinary man, this phrase came to mind, perhaps because of its Messianic connotations. The disciples' reaction here does not upstage Peter's deliberately Christological use of the title in 16:16, but prepares the way for it" (R.T. France).

the Son of God. In the Old Testament, this term was used to describe God's appointed king who was to reign over Israel in God's stead (e.g., Ps. 2:7). In the New Testament, the title is often used in connection with the title "Messiah." This scene highlights Jesus' divine appointment as God's representative and king since he exhibits the very power and authority of God.

14:36 the edge of his cloak. This recalls the healing of the woman in Mark 5:25–28. Jesus was so powerful that even touching the very edge of his garment, i.e., making the most minimal contact with him, was sufficient to experience that power.

UNIT 10—Two Blind Miracle Stories / Mark 8:22-26; 10:46-52

The Healing of a Blind Man at Bethsaida

²²**They came to Bethsaida, and some people brought a blind man and begged Jesus to touch him. ²³He took the blind man by the hand and led him outside the village. When he had spit on the man's eyes and put his hands on him, Jesus asked, "Do you see anything?"**

²⁴**He looked up and said, "I see people; they look like trees walking around."**

²⁵**Once more Jesus put his hands on the man's eyes. Then his eyes were opened, his sight was restored, and he saw everything clearly. ²⁶Jesus sent him home, saying, "Don't go into the village." ...**

Blind Bartimaeus Receives His Sight

⁴⁶**Then they came to Jericho. As Jesus and his disciples, together with a large crowd, were leaving the city, a blind man, Bartimaeus (that is, the Son of Timaeus), was sitting by the roadside begging. ⁴⁷When he heard that it was Jesus of Nazareth, he began to shout, "Jesus, Son of David, have mercy on me!"**

⁴⁸**Many rebuked him and told him to be quiet, but he shouted all the more, "Son of David, have mercy on me!"**

⁴⁹**Jesus stopped and said, "Call him."**

So they called to the blind man, "Cheer up! On your feet! He's calling you." ⁵⁰Throwing his cloak aside, he jumped to his feet and came to Jesus.

⁵¹**"What do you want me to do for you?" Jesus asked him.**

The blind man said, "Rabbi, I want to see."

⁵²**"Go," said Jesus, "your faith has healed you." Immediately he received his sight and followed Jesus along the road.**

READ
First Reading / First Impressions: What question from these stories stands out to you the most?
- ❐ Why did Jesus lead the blind man outside the village (8:23) and then tell him not to go back to the village (8:26)?
- ❐ Why did Jesus spit on the man's eyes (8:23)?
- ❐ Why was this instance of healing gradual (8:24–25)?
- ❐ Why did the crowd rebuke Bartimaeus and tell him to be quiet (10:48)?
- ❐ Why did Jesus ask a blind person what he wanted Jesus to do for him (10:51)?
- ❐ other:_____

Second Reading / Big Idea: What do you assume at this point to be Mark's reason for telling these stories?

SEARCH
1. Why do you suppose Jesus spit on the blind man's eyes (8:23)?

2. In what ways does the limited healing of the blind man in 8:24 prepare the way for how the disciples perceive Jesus in Mark 8:27–33? In what way is their spiritual sight partial, and when is their sight clarified (see Summary note for 8:22–26)?

48

3. The story of Bartimaeus immediately follows the story of how James and John maneuvered to try to get the chief places in Jesus' kingdom (Mark 10:35–45). How do Bartimaeus' words and deeds serve as an example, even to the Twelve (see notes, especially on 10:52)?

4. The first story is the final miracle before Peter's climactic confession that Jesus is the Christ (Mark 8:29). The second story is the final miracle Jesus performs before entering Jerusalem to be crucified. What might be Mark's point in placing these two miracles of sight just prior to two major events in Jesus' ministry?

APPLY

1. When it comes to your understanding of Jesus at this point, what would you say you are?
   ❒ I'm blind—I haven't a clue who he really is.
   ❒ I have partial sight—I think I can make out some of who he is, but it's still really fuzzy.
   ❒ I have clear vision—I am sure I know who he is now.

2. In the second story, the blind man "sees" in a way the disciples and the crowd do not. With which character(s) do you identify right now?
   ❒ the disciples—I'm afraid that most of the time I'm still mainly concerned about securing my own status in life.
   ❒ the crowd—I hate it when someone interferes with my idea of how God ought to act.
   ❒ Bartimaeus—I've come to the point where nothing or no one is going to keep me from pursuing Jesus.

Why did you pick the character(s) you did?

3. In what area of your life would you like Jesus to open your eyes so you could see more clearly?

GROUP AGENDA

After the first part, read the Scripture out loud and divide into groups of 4. Then come back together for the third part.

TO BEGIN / 10–15 Min. (Choose 1 or 2)

1. If you wear glasses or contacts, how did you (or someone else) first realize your vision wasn't right?

2. If you completely lost your sight, what would you miss seeing the most?

3. How do you respond when a beggar approaches you on the street? Why?

TO GO DEEPER / 30 Min. (Choose 2 or 3)

1. In doing the homework assignment, what stood out to you the most from this passage or the study notes?

2. In the first story, what is Jesus' point in healing the man in stages? When have you experienced a gradual miracle in your life or in someone close to you?

3. What is significant about the way Bartimaeus addresses Jesus (see notes on 10:47)?

4. Why do you think Jesus asked Bartimaeus, who was obviously blind, "What do you want me to do for you?"

5. CASE STUDY: Rajiv is a young student from India who is studying in the United States and got interested in your Bible study group. He recently made a commitment to Jesus Christ, and has many questions. In reading the stories of Jesus' miracles, he asks you what the role of Jesus, of faith, and of prayer is in healing today. How do you answer Rajiv?

TO CLOSE / 15–30 Min.

1. How are you doing on your group mission?

2. How did you answer the questions in APPLY, especially the third question?

3. If Jesus asked you today, "What do you want me to do for you?" what would you say?

4. How would you like the group to pray for you this week?

NOTES

Summary for 8:22–26. There are clear parallels between this healing and the healing of the deaf and mute man in Mark 7:31–37. It is almost certain that Mark regarded them as forming a pair. He has placed them in parallel positions in relation to the two feeding miracles and both concern healings promised in Isaiah 35:5–6. Jesus had just admonished the Twelve for their spiritual blindness and deafness (Mark 8:17–18). The "blind" disciples are about to receive their "first touch" of healing, for in the next scene Peter will declare that they know that Jesus is the Messiah (8:27–30). This is a great step forward in their understanding, however Peter's vigorous rejection of Jesus' teaching about his death demonstrates they have not fully understood what he is about (Mark 8:31–33). They need a "second touch" to open their eyes completely. This will not come until Jesus dies and rises again.

8:22 *Bethsaida.* This was a town at the mouth of the Jordan River on the shore of the Sea of Galilee.

8:23 *led him outside the village.* While some of Jesus' miracles were performed in full view of people, others were acts of compassion done privately. In those cases, Jesus told the people involved not to tell others what had happened (see v. 26; Mark 1:44; 3:12; 5:43). This may be due to the fact he did not wish to fuel premature and misdirected expectations about what he, as the Messiah, was going to do.

When he had spit on the man's eyes and put his hands on him. Since most of Jesus' miracles were accomplished simply by a word, it is unclear why this was necessary. Since such actions were involved in other Jewish healing practices, it may be that Jesus used this means as a way to enter into the thought world of the blind man (Lane). This is what the man (and the onlookers) would have expected a healer to do.

8:24 *they look like trees.* The man's sight is improved, but not enough so he could function as a person whose vision is good. He had probably once been sighted since he knows what a tree looks like.

8:25 *Once more.* This is the only healing that requires a second action on the part of Jesus. Mark's placement of this story right after the disciples' incomprehension of the meaning of the feeding miracles, and just prior to their confession of faith in him as the Messiah, indicates he is using this story to illustrate how difficult it was for the disciples to grasp Jesus' identity.

8:26 *Don't go into the village.* The man apparently lived outside of the town itself but would go there daily to beg. This is understood to be another call for silence (see note on 8:23).

Summary for 10:46–52. While both these stories involve the healing of a blind man, the point of each story is quite different. The first story accented the blindness of the disciples in terms of understanding who Jesus is. This story accents the identity of Jesus as the messianic Son of David come to free those who trust him. Happening just prior to Jesus' final entry into Jerusalem, it is a demonstration of faith that stands in stark contrast to the determined resistance and opposition Jesus will soon face. This story may also be intended as a reminder of the earlier one in that it follows a scene where the disciples have again demonstrated that they really do not understand the nature of Jesus and his kingdom (Mark 10:35–45). They are still blind or, at best, have only partial sight.

10:46 *Jericho.* They have almost completed their journey from Galilee (see Mark 9:33; 10:1). Jericho is a city about 15 miles east of Jerusalem and the place where travelers recrossed the Jordan back into Israel. It was the site of Herod's magnificent winter palace and the home of many of the priests that served in the temple in Jerusalem.

a large crowd. These were pilgrims on their way to Jerusalem for the Passover Feast. Every male over 12 years of age living within a 15-mile radius of Jerusalem was expected to attend. Many Jews from throughout the Roman Empire and the East would likewise try to visit Jerusalem during Passover.

10:47 *Jesus, Son of David.* This is the only time in Mark's Gospel that this title is used of Jesus, although Matthew and Luke use it quite often. At the time of Jesus it was sometimes used as a title of respect for someone perceived to be particularly blessed by God. However, its occurrence at this point in the narrative (just prior to Jesus' death) indicates Mark wanted it to be understood as a messianic title. Although the religious leaders fail to see who he is, the blind (who were often thought to be blind because of some especially bad sin they had committed) do see. Not only that, they receive their sight as was prophesied would happen when the time of God's redemption drew near (Isa. 35:5). While Jesus told the man in chapter 8 not to tell what had happened, here Jesus lets the statement of Bartimaeus stand. He accepts the title. The time

for secrecy is past. From now on he would be recognized as the messianic King.

have mercy on me. This is the cry of the psalmists to God for deliverance (Ps. 4:1; 6:2; 51:1; 109:26; 123:3). Bartimaeus recognizes Jesus as the agent of God through whom his deliverance would come. This may be intended as a model prayer for the Christian community: a recognition of Jesus' divine identity and a simple plea for mercy. The story shows it is a prayer Jesus is eager to answer.

10:48 *Many rebuked him.* Whether the rebuke was for what he said or because people resented his shouting or because people assumed he was too insignificant to be bothered with by a man as great as Jesus is uncertain.

he shouted all the more. His faith had latched on to Jesus and he would not be deterred.

10:50 *Throwing his cloak aside.* This would have been his garment which was probably laid in front of him upon which he gathered alms. His casting it aside so that it would not get in his way of getting to Jesus indicates his single-minded determination. If he was not healed, there would be no guarantee that he, a blind man, would find it again. The coins he had collected upon it would be scattered among the crowd and lost. This is a picture of someone forsaking all to come after Jesus (see Mark 8:34).

10:51 Although his need was obvious, the fact that he must declare it shows his conviction that Jesus can heal him.

Rabbi. This means "Rabboni," a title of more honor and respect than "Rabbi." It means "*my* master" or "*my* lord," a further indication of Bartimaeus' faith.

10:52 *your faith has healed you.* See also Mark 2:5 and 5:34. This healing was not a matter of impersonal power, but of a relationship of faith in One who is compassionate and gracious. Blind Bartimaeus demonstrated his faith in several ways: by the title he uses for Jesus (showing that he grasped who Jesus was), by his persistence in calling and immediately jumping up and going to Jesus (he will not let this opportunity go by), and by his request for healing (showing that he believed Jesus could do so).

followed Jesus. His healing freed him to become a disciple. Likewise, as the Twelve become fully aware of Jesus' nature and mission, they too will be expected to follow in his way.

UNIT 11—Lazarus / John 11:1-3,17-27,38-47

The Death of Lazarus

11 **Now a man named Lazarus was sick. He was from Bethany, the village of Mary and her sister Martha. ²This Mary, whose brother Lazarus now lay sick, was the same one who poured perfume on the Lord and wiped his feet with her hair. ³So the sisters sent word to Jesus, "Lord, the one you love is sick." ...**

Jesus Comforts the Sisters

¹⁷On his arrival, Jesus found that Lazarus had already been in the tomb for four days. ¹⁸Bethany was less than two milesᵃ **from Jerusalem, ¹⁹and many Jews had come to Martha and Mary to comfort them in the loss of their brother. ²⁰When Martha heard that Jesus was coming, she went out to meet him, but Mary stayed at home.**

²¹"Lord," Martha said to Jesus, "if you had been here, my brother would not have died. ²²But I know that even now God will give you whatever you ask."

²³Jesus said to her, "Your brother will rise again."

²⁴Martha answered, "I know he will rise again in the resurrection at the last day."

²⁵Jesus said to her, "I am the resurrection and the life. He who believes in me will live, even though he dies; ²⁶and whoever lives and believes in me will never die. Do you believe this?"

²⁷"Yes, Lord," she told him, "I believe that you are the Christ,ᵇ **the Son of God, who was to come into the world." ...**

Jesus Raises Lazarus From the Dead

³⁸Jesus, once more deeply moved, came to the tomb. It was a cave with a stone laid across the entrance. ³⁹"Take away the stone," he said.

"But, Lord," said Martha, the sister of the dead man, "by this time there is a bad odor, for he has been there four days."

⁴⁰Then Jesus said, "Did I not tell you that if you believed, you would see the glory of God?"

⁴¹So they took away the stone. Then Jesus looked up and said, "Father, I thank you that you have heard me. ⁴²I knew that you always hear me, but I said this for the benefit of the people standing here, that they may believe that you sent me."

⁴³When he had said this, Jesus called in a loud voice, "Lazarus, come out!" ⁴⁴The dead man came out, his hands and feet wrapped with strips of linen, and a cloth around his face.

Jesus said to them, "Take off the grave clothes and let him go."

⁴⁵Therefore many of the Jews who had come to visit Mary, and had seen what Jesus did, put their faith in him. ⁴⁶But some of them went to the Pharisees and told them what Jesus had done. ⁴⁷Then the chief priests and the Pharisees called a meeting of the Sanhedrin.

ᵃ18 Greek *fifteen stadia* (about 3 kilometers)   ᵇ27 Or *Messiah*

READ

First Reading / First Impressions: Since Jesus didn't come right away when he received the sisters' message, Lazarus had been dead four days when Jesus arrived. How would you feel if you were Mary or Martha and heard that Jesus had finally come?

❑ despondent—It's too late.

❑ angry—It's about time!

❑ consoled—Better late than never.

❑ hopeful—With Jesus, it's never too late.

Second Reading / Big Idea: Write a short title that captures the central meaning of this story.

SEARCH

1. What was Jesus' relationship with Lazarus and his sisters (see second note on v. 3)?

52

2. This is the final, climactic miracle in John's Gospel—through which the author communicates a great deal about Jesus. What insights about Jesus do you see from the following?

Jesus' comments in verses 25–26 (see notes):

Martha's response in verse 27 (see notes):

Jesus' emotional state in verse 38 (see also John 11:32–35):

Jesus' actions in verses 41–44 (see notes):

APPLY

1. The raising of Lazarus illustrates both the future resurrection and the present new birth that all believers experience (see John 3:7; 5:25,28–29). Using that analogy, how would you describe your state at this point?
   ❏ I think I'm still dead in the tomb.
   ❏ I've been raised, but the grave clothes are bound so tight I still can't move much.
   ❏ I am being relieved of the old grave clothes and am finally really living!
   ❏ other:_____

2. Are there some old grave clothes that still need to be shed for you to be completely free in Christ? If so, what are they?

3. How can the hope of a heavenly life positively affect the way you live your earthly life?

GROUP AGENDA

After the first part, read the Scripture out loud and divide into groups of 4. Then come back together for the third part.

TO BEGIN / 10–15 Min. (Choose 1 or 2)
1. When was the last time you attended a funeral? What was it like?

2. Who is the closest person to you who has died or is dying?

3. How do you express your feelings when you are in the midst of crises or grief?

TO GO DEEPER / 30 Min. (Choose 2 or 3)
1. Briefly go through as many of the READ and SEARCH questions as you can.

2. If Martha had faith in Jesus (v. 22), why was she skeptical when Jesus asked for the stone to be removed from the entrance to the tomb (v. 39)?

3. Why did Jesus raise Lazarus from the dead?

4. How do people you know who don't believe in Christ and the resurrection react when someone they care for dies? How strongly do *you* believe verses 25–26?

5. How could you use this story to help a person who is facing death?

6. CASE STUDY: Lisa has been active in church all her life and always felt that she had a strong and sincere faith. But her life is falling apart. Her mother died of cancer six months ago. Last month Lisa had a miscarriage. And her stress at work is becoming unbearable. She confesses to you: "I'm having a hard time even believing in God. Where has he been during the last six months? If God really loves me, how could he let me hurt like this?" What can you say or do?

TO CLOSE / 15–30 Min.
1. How did your group answer the three "Brainstorming" questions on page M19 in the center section?

2. Share your answer to at least one of the questions in APPLY.

3. How has this group helped to unwrap the grave clothes in your life and set you free?

4. What still holds you in bondage that this group can pray about?

54

NOTES

Summary. In the Gospel of John this is the last of the seven signs of Jesus' glory which John records (2:1–11; 4:46–54; 5:1–11; 6:1–13,16–20; 9:1–7). It serves both to enact the truth Jesus taught concerning his power to give life (John 5:28–30) and to foreshadow his own death and resurrection.

11:2 *Mary ... who poured perfume on the Lord.* Apparently John, aware that the story of Jesus' anointing was a familiar one to his readers (see Mark 14:1–11), used this incident to identify Mary even though it doesn't occur in his Gospel until chapter 12.

11:3 Given Jesus' reputation as a healer it is not surprising that the sisters would send for him when their brother fell ill.

the one you love. Jesus was a friend to Lazarus and his sisters (see Luke 10:38–42). Not only do the sisters remark on the love Jesus had for Lazarus, but so do the villagers when they see that Jesus is moved to tears at the tomb of Lazarus (John 11:33–36). The only other person who is identified as "one whom Jesus loved" is the writer of this Gospel (John 13:23–25; 21:20–24).

11:17 *four days.* Since Jesus' journey was probably only a day's length at most, Lazarus must have died the day Jesus received the message, but after it was already sent. There was a notion that up until the third day a person's spirit hovered over the body allowing for the hope of recovery, but after that no hope was possible. In light of this belief, Jesus' delay may have been to disavow any expectation that recovery could be possible. The mourning ceremonies reached their crescendo on the fourth day.

11:19 *many Jews.* The author accents the size of the crowd to show that this final public sign was seen by many.

11:21 *if you had been here, my brother would not have died.* Since Lazarus had died probably even before Jesus received the message, this is not a rebuke but an expression of regret. It implies faith that if Jesus had been on the scene before his death, Lazarus could have been saved.

11:22 *But I know.* Given her confusion in verse 39, when Jesus asks for the tomb to be opened, this is not an expectation that Jesus could do a miracle even now, but an expression of her belief that Jesus, had he been on the scene, could have healed Lazarus since "God will give you whatever you ask."

11:23 *will rise again.* The Pharisees and other Jewish groups believed in a general resurrection. She would have understood Jesus' comment as simply an appropriate expression of comfort at a funeral.

11:25 *I am the resurrection and the life.* This claim would jar anyone at a funeral! By it Jesus focuses Martha's attention, not on the doctrine of the general resurrection, but on him as the source of that resurrection. This is a personalized way of expressing the truth he taught in more abstract terms in John 5:24–29.

will live, even though he dies. Spiritual life that will not end at physical death is in view here. In this verse and in verse 26, Jesus is asserting his sovereign power over death and his ability to "give life to whom he is pleased to give it" (John 5:21). Given this framework, the actual resurrection of Lazarus will be a dramatic sign of the validity of his claim.

11:26 *Do you believe this?* Jesus directly confronts Martha with this claim. Does she see him only as a healer or as the Lord of life?

11:27 *Lord.* This term can mean simply "Sir," a polite form of address. Whereas in verse 21 it may have that intent, in this verse the author is using it in its sense as a title for deity since the rest of Martha's statement is full of spiritual insight into his identity.

Christ, the Son of God, who was to come into the world. This threefold declaration is one of several "confessional" statements about Jesus that the author weaves into his narrative which reflect the conclusions he wants his readers to draw about Jesus (see John 6:69; 16:30; 20:28). In calling him the Christ (the Greek term for Messiah), Martha acknowledges Jesus as the One who delivers and saves his people from the power of sin and death. Her recognition of him as the Son of God shows her insight into his divine identity. The meaning behind this title is that he is "just like" God, sharing God's essential nature just as a child shares the characteristics of his or her parents. The final phrase, "who was to come into the world," refers to the expectation that one day a leader like Moses would arise (Deut. 18:18). This too acknowledges his authority and divine commission.

11:38 *the tomb.* Tombs for people of importance were either vertical shafts or horizontal hollows, both covered by a stone. Since this tomb is carved out of a cave, it would probably be the former type.

11:39 *bad odor.* Even if Martha knew of the others Jesus had raised (see Matt. 11:5; Mark 5:22–43; Luke 7:11–15), they were people who had been dead for only a short time. By the fourth day the actual decomposition of the body had begun and therefore no resuscitation could be possible.

11:40 *Did I not tell you.* This may be a reference to Jesus' response to the message in 11:4, or the implication of what he meant by his declaration to Martha in verse 25. The irony is that it is this final sign, which demonstrates his glory far more than any of the other signs, that finally leads the religious authorities to take specific steps to put him to death (John 11:53).

the glory of God. There is a double meaning here. The act of raising Lazarus from the dead would obviously be a divine act of power, for only God can give life; yet the signs have consistently been regarded as demonstrations of Jesus' identity. They reveal his glory (John 2:11), and based on them people make decisions about who he is (John 6:14; 9:33). This final sign will reveal what has been alluded to all along—Jesus is divine. He shares the power and nature of the Father. What the prologue described in abstract terms (John 1:1–3) will be clearly shown here.

11:41 *looked up.* This was a common posture for prayer.

11:42 *that they may believe that you sent me.* Lazarus' resurrection was to be a powerful sign of the Father's stamp of approval upon Jesus.

11:44 *The dead man came out.* Through this humorous phrase, the author provides a foretaste of the experience all people will share at the final resurrection when "all who are in their graves will hear (Jesus') voice and come out" (John 5:28–29).

wrapped with strips of linen. While burial customs included wrapping the body with cloth and spices (John 19:40), this was not intended to preserve the body like the ancient Egyptian process of mummification.

grave clothes. Lazarus' resuscitation differs from Jesus' resurrection in that his grave clothes were still with him. He would still need them at some later time. In contrast, Jesus' grave clothes were left behind in the tomb, never to be needed again (John 20:6–8). Lazarus' coming to life only robbed death for a time; Jesus' resurrection spells the ultimate defeat of death's power.

UNIT 12—The Withered Fig Tree / Mark 11:12-25

Jesus Clears the Temple

¹²The next day as they were leaving Bethany, Jesus was hungry. ¹³Seeing in the distance a fig tree in leaf, he went to find out if it had any fruit. When he reached it, he found nothing but leaves, because it was not the season for figs. ¹⁴Then he said to the tree, "May no one ever eat fruit from you again." And his disciples heard him say it.

¹⁵On reaching Jerusalem, Jesus entered the temple area and began driving out those who were buying and selling there. He overturned the tables of the money changers and the benches of those selling doves, ¹⁶and would not allow anyone to carry merchandise through the temple courts. ¹⁷And as he taught them, he said, "Is it not written:

" 'My house will be called
a house of prayer for all nations'ᵃ?

But you have made it a 'den of robbers.'ᵇ"

¹⁸The chief priests and the teachers of the law heard this and began looking for a way to kill him, for they feared him, because the whole crowd was amazed at his teaching.

¹⁹When evening came, theyᶜ went out of the city.

The Withered Fig Tree

²⁰In the morning, as they went along, they saw the fig tree withered from the roots. ²¹Peter remembered and said to Jesus, "Rabbi, look! The fig tree you cursed has withered!"

²²"Haveᵈ faith in God," Jesus answered. ²³"I tell you the truth, if anyone says to this mountain, 'Go, throw yourself into the sea,' and does not doubt in his heart but believes that what he says will happen, it will be done for him. ²⁴Therefore I tell you, whatever you ask for in prayer, believe that you have received it, and it will be yours. ²⁵And when you stand praying, if you hold anything against anyone, forgive him, so that your Father in heaven may forgive you your sins.ᵉ"

ᵃ17 Isaiah 56:7   ᵇ17 Jer. 7:11
ᶜ19 Some early manuscripts *he*   ᵈ22 Some early manuscripts *If you have*   ᵉ25 Some manuscripts *sins.*

READ
First Reading / First Impressions: As a quick, first impression, how surprising is it to you to read of Jesus cursing a fig tree and overturning tables and benches in the temple?

❏ very surprising   ❏ a little surprising   ❏ not surprising at all

Second Reading / Big Idea: How would you sum up what seems to be the point of this passage?

SEARCH
1. Given what you know about the situation of the religious leaders at the time of Jesus, what parallels do you see between them and the fig tree in verse 13?

2. What do you think is Mark's purpose in sandwiching the story of the cleansing of the temple between the two scenes involving the fig tree (see Jer. 7:9–15; 8:13; and note on v. 20)?

3. What qualities stand out to you about Jesus from these scenes?

4. How does the miracle of the withered fig tree serve as a springboard to Jesus' teaching about faith and prayer (see notes on 11:22–26 and 11:23–24)?

5. What conditions for effective prayer are raised in verses 22–25?

APPLY

1. Give an example of what you think is a right application of the promises in verses 22–24. What is an example of a wrong application?

2. Compared to a fig tree, where are you these days spiritually?
   ❏ a new shoot—I'm just starting out, there's not much to judge yet!
   ❏ in full leaf—The foliage looks good, but I'm afraid there's no real fruit being produced.
   ❏ bearing fruit—There is some clear evidence I can point to of growth in my obedience to God.
   ❏ picked clean—Last year I did okay, but there's not much happening now.

3. What would have to change in order for you to be more fruitful?
   ❏ I need to take in more of God's sun and water.
   ❏ I need to be pruned to get rid of nonproductive branches that are draining me.
   ❏ I need to be transplanted into a more supportive environment.
   ❏ I need to quit being concerned about the foliage and start producing fruit!
   ❏ other:_____

   What is one step you could take toward becoming more fruitful?

GROUP AGENDA

After the first part, read the Scripture out loud and divide into groups of 4. Then come back together for the third part.

TO BEGIN / 10–15 Min. (Choose 1 or 2)

1. What fruit or vegetable would you be glad to never eat again?

2. What does it take to get you to clean your home?

3. When you see something wrong, do you tend to act without thinking or think without acting?

TO GO DEEPER / 30 Min. (Choose 2 or 3)

1. Based on the homework and the study notes, how would you summarize the major points of this passage and what's going on behind the scenes?

2. In what ways can you recall the Pharisees covering their fruitlessness with flashy foliage?

3. How do you feel about expressing anger? Have you ever expressed righteous anger? When?

4. If you could change one thing about modern Christianity, what would it be? What have you done to make your church a better place?

5. What amazing answer to prayer can you remember receiving? How much faith did it take?

6. CASE STUDY: You are regretting your decision to accept your church's request to be a small group leader! Throughout your group's study of Jesus' miracles, Gary and Stan have gotten into arguments. Gary thinks that Christians should expect the same kind of miracles that your group has been studying, and the fact that they don't is a sign of apathy—if not apostasy. Stan thinks that Jesus' miracles were basically meant to communicate who he was, and that Christians today should no longer seek after such signs and wonders. What can you do about this dilemma?

TO CLOSE / 15–30 Min.

1. Are you planning a kickoff for starting a new small group? Have you made plans for celebrating your time together as a group?

2. Share your answer to at least one question in APPLY.

3. What keeps you from making your life more of a "house of prayer"?

4. How would you like the group to pray for you?

NOTES

Summary. The cursing and withering of the fig tree is the only incident of a miracle that is destructive in nature. Between the curse (v. 14) and its withering (v. 20), Mark sandwiches the story of the cleansing of the temple. Each story helps interpret the other. Both illustrate the judgment that is coming on Jerusalem. The disciples surprise upon discovering the withered fig tree leads into a discussion about faith and prayer.

11:13 *fig tree.* On the Mount of Olives fig trees are in leaf by early April but they would not have ripe fruit until June, long after the Passover. Fig trees were a common prophetic symbol associated with Israel and with judgment (e.g., Jer. 8:13; Hosea 9:10; Micah 7:1). Thus, it was no accident that Jesus chose a fig tree for this particular drama.

11:14 *his disciples heard him say it.* Jesus has done something so seemingly out of character (cursing a fig tree for not doing what it could not do) that the disciples cannot help but notice. Since there is no obvious reason for his action (Mark has taken care to point out that "it was not the season for figs"), they are forced to ponder why he did this. This, of course, was his intention. In the same way that he often used extravagant language to make his point (e.g. Mark 9:42–43), here Jesus uses extravagant actions to get across this crucial point. Such acted-out parables were very much a part of how the Old Testament prophets communicated (e.g., Isa. 20; Ezek. 4–5).

11:15–19 Jesus' first act following his triumphal entry is to go into the temple and, by his actions, call to account the religious leadership of Israel. It is significant that he challenges these leaders in the temple, the very center of their power. For the second time, Jesus conveys his message by means of dramatic action. Jesus' action in the temple would have shocked everyone as he totally disrupted "normal" business and drastically interfered in religious observances.

11:15 *buying and selling.* The system of worship in the temple was built around sacrifice. The actual act of selling the animals in the temple area was not in itself a problem since this had originally been instituted as a means of assisting Jewish pilgrims who had to travel long distances to come to Jerusalem. Since they could obtain an animal for sacrifice at the temple, they would not have to deal with the problems of having a lamb traveling with them. However, by this time what once was a helpful service had become a racket. People could only offer an unblemished animal as a sacrifice and the animal had to be inspected first. Apparently, the temple inspectors approved only those animals bought from certified vendors who sold the animals at a huge markup. These merchants actually worked for members of the high priest's family. As a result, the priests, the merchants and the inspectors all made a profit by taking advantage of the religious obligations of the Jewish people.

money changers. At Passover each Jew was required to pay a temple tax of one-half shekel (nearly two days' wages). No other currency was acceptable, necessitating money changers to exchange the money of pilgrims coming from outside Jerusalem. The money changers, however, charged exorbitant amounts for the simple act of exchanging currency: up to one-half day's wages of working people.

those selling doves. Temple vendors charged 20 times what it cost to buy a dove outside the temple.

11:16 carry merchandise. Merchants used the temple court as a convenient walkway from one part of the city to another. Rather than respecting the sanctity of the temple by carrying their wares around it, they simply walked on through.

11:17 a house of prayer for all nations. This is a quote from Isaiah 56:7. Isaiah had a vision of the temple as a gathering place where all types of people might gather in common, reverent, joyful worship of God. The outermost area of the temple where all these activities were taking place was called the Court of the Gentiles since it was the only part of the temple Gentiles could enter (the other sections of the temple were reserved only for Jews). Instead of pursuing Isaiah's vision, the temple authorities had allowed this court to be turned into a raucous oriental bazaar, making prayer impossible.

den of robbers. This is a quote from Jeremiah 7:11 where God rebukes the religious authorities of that day for using religion as a cloak for injustice.

11:18 The chief priests were Sadducees, and the teachers of the Law were typically Pharisees. The two sects normally did not cooperate together since they had so many differences between them, but they acted as one in their decision regarding Jesus. Rather than responding with repentance, the religious leaders plotted how to kill Jesus. Their concern was that the people might listen to him, resist

their leadership, and revolt against their system.

11:19 they went out of the city. Pilgrims coming to Jerusalem for Passover would often stay outside the city at night.

11:20 the fig tree withered from the roots. In light of the cleansing of the temple, the meaning of the withered fig tree becomes clear. This is what will happen to Israel. Judgment is coming on Jerusalem and on the temple in particular. "Just as the leaves of the tree concealed the fact that there was no fruit to enjoy, so too the magnificence of the Temple and its ceremony conceals the fact that Israel has not brought forth the fruit of righteousness demanded by God" (Lane; see also Mark 7:6). The fig tree's fate will be the temple's fate. The temple was, in fact, destroyed by the Romans in A.D. 70 after a violent Jewish revolt against the empire. It has never been rebuilt.

11:22–26 As he has done several times in his Gospel (see 4:21–34; 9:42–50), Mark adds to the main story a group of similar sayings (this time on the subject of faith and prayer). While the miracle itself is a sign of the judgment to come upon Israel, these verses use it as an example of prayer's effectiveness.

11:23–24 This is another example of Jesus' use of extravagant language. He cannot literally and mechanically mean that whatever is asked will happen since that would turn prayer into magic and God into a cosmic bellhop attending to the whim of even evil and selfish people. Still, the point is not to be missed: believing prayer, based in confidence of God's power and purposes, is answered. The point is not that Jesus promises his disciples the power to do massive earthmoving feats through prayer, but that seemingly impossible obstacles (such as the resistance of the religious authorities to the message of Jesus) in the way of God's plan can be overcome through faith and prayer.

11:23 this mountain ... into the sea. This is probably the Mount of Olives overlooking Jerusalem. The Dead Sea is visible from the Mount of Olives.

11:25 See also Matthew 6:12–14. These types of commands are not meant to encourage a sense of bargaining with God, as if the disciple is to wring forgiveness out of God by making sure he or she is not holding a grudge against anyone else. Such commands simply are a reflection that the recognition of our great debt before God is what moves us to freely forgive those who have sinned against us.

UNIT 13—The Catch of Fish / John 21:1-14

Jesus and the Miraculous Catch of Fish

21 Afterward Jesus appeared again to his disciples, by the Sea of Tiberias.[a] It happened this way: ²Simon Peter, Thomas (called Didymus), Nathanael from Cana in Galilee, the sons of Zebedee, and two other disciples were together. ³"I'm going out to fish," Simon Peter told them, and they said, "We'll go with you." So they went out and got into the boat, but that night they caught nothing.

⁴Early in the morning, Jesus stood on the shore, but the disciples did not realize that it was Jesus.

⁵He called out to them, "Friends, haven't you any fish?"

"No," they answered.

⁶He said, "Throw your net on the right side of the boat and you will find some." When they did, they were unable to haul the net in because of the large number of fish.

⁷Then the disciple whom Jesus loved said to Peter, "It is the Lord!" As soon as Simon Peter heard him say, "It is the Lord," he wrapped his outer garment around him (for he had taken it off) and jumped into the water. ⁸The other disciples followed in the boat, towing the net full of fish, for they were not far from shore, about a hundred yards.[b] ⁹When they landed, they saw a fire of burning coals there with fish on it, and some bread.

¹⁰Jesus said to them, "Bring some of the fish you have just caught."

¹¹Simon Peter climbed aboard and dragged the net ashore. It was full of large fish, 153, but even with so many the net was not torn. ¹²Jesus said to them, "Come and have breakfast." None of the disciples dared ask him, "Who are you?" They knew it was the Lord. ¹³Jesus came, took the bread and gave it to them, and did the same with the fish. ¹⁴This was now the third time Jesus appeared to his disciples after he was raised from the dead.

[a]1 That is, Sea of Galilee [b]8 Greek *about two hundred cubits* (about 90 meters)

READ

First Reading / First Impressions: What strikes you as the point of this "fish story"?

Second Reading / Big Idea: What is one question this story raises in your mind that you hope further reflection will help you answer?

SEARCH

1. Why do you think Peter and the other disciples went back to Peter's home territory of Galilee?
   - ❐ to relax and to do some fishing
   - ❐ to go back to their old occupation
   - ❐ to put their lives back together
   - ❐ to forget about Jesus
   - ❐ to obey Jesus' instructions to go to Galilee and wait for him there

2. Why did Jesus' followers have difficulty recognizing him (v. 4; see note)?

3. Compare this story with that in Luke 5:1–11. What similarities and differences do you see? Since the fish were apparently not needed for food (see v. 9), what was this miracle intended to symbolize for the disciples (see first note on v. 3)?

4. What effect might the repetition of this miracle have on Peter, especially in light of his denial (John 18:17,25–27)?

5. What connection do you see between this story and the Lord's Supper (see note on v. 13)?

6. According to the note on verse 14, why are Jesus' post-resurrection appearances so important?

APPLY

1. What effect has this course had on your perspective of Jesus and his miracles? What has this study done for your faith?

2. When it comes to understanding Jesus' call upon your life now, are you still "fishing in the dark" (v. 3) or meeting with him in the light of dawn (vv. 12–13)? Why do you answer as you do? What is the next step for you?

GROUP AGENDA

After the first part, read the Scripture out loud and divide into groups of 4. Then come back together for the third part.

TO BEGIN / 10–15 Min. (Choose 1 or 2)
1. What is the biggest fish you have ever caught?

2. What is your favorite food on a cookout?

3. What is the sweetest reunion you've ever had with family or friends?

TO GO DEEPER / 30 Min. (Choose 2 or 3)
1. If you were Peter and knew you had just recently blown it by denying Jesus, how would you be feeling about the miraculous catch of fish and the breakfast Jesus served?

2. Based on the SEARCH questions and the study notes, what do you see as Jesus' purpose in providing a miraculous catch of fish and then making breakfast for these disciples?

3. What is the closest you have come to "throwing in the towel" and going back on your promise to follow Jesus? How did Jesus meet you in this experience and bring you back?

4. How would you explain the importance of Jesus' resurrection to a non-Christian?

5. What difference does the resurrection of Christ and your own future resurrection make in the way you live your life today?

6. CASE STUDY: A couple of people in your group are having a very difficult time dealing with their past. Harold blames himself for the recent failure of his business and feels very guilty for the financial repercussions this is having on his family. Joyce had an affair resulting in her divorce a couple of years ago and can't forgive herself. How can the stories of Jesus' miracles in general, and Peter's story in particular, help Harold and Joyce?

TO CLOSE / 15 –30 Min.
1. How did you answer the questions in APPLY?

2. What have you appreciated the most about this study and this group?

3. Have you finalized your plans for the future of your group?

4. How can the group remember you in prayer?

NOTES

Summary. Jesus rose from the dead. He then appeared to his disciples—alive, recognizable, and full of power. He was no ghost. He had a body. He ate with others. But it was a different kind of body. He came through locked doors (John 20:19). He walked with his followers and yet they did not at first recognize him (Luke 24:13–32). His was a resurrection body. In this account, the resurrected Jesus meets once again with his disciples.

There are two miracles in this account: the huge catch of fish and the appearance of Jesus who had been crucified. The first miracle is what we have come to expect from Jesus: He has power over nature. For him to bring about a spectacular catch of fish is in line with his other miracles (and he had done this once before, see Luke 5:1–11). The second miracle is the extraordinary one. For him to rise from the dead and appear to his disciples is one of the greatest of all miracles.

Some scholars feel that chapter 21 functions like an appendix to the Gospel of John, focusing on the disciples and thus forming a bridge from the life of Jesus into the ministry of the church. And certainly, John 20:30–31 sounds like a concluding statement. However, chapter 21 is clearly connected with what precedes it. It begins with the phrase, "Afterward Jesus appeared again to his disciples." And in verse 14 we learn that this is the third post-resurrection appearance by Jesus to his disciples, thus linking this chapter to the two previous appearances (John 20:19–23; 26–29). There is the same startled and joyous acclamation one finds at other appearances. Peter declares in verse 7, "It is the Lord!" just as Mary exclaimed, "I have seen the Lord!" (John 20:18) and Thomas professed, "My Lord and my God!" (John 20:28).

21:1 Afterward. Literally, this is "after these things." We do not know how long after the Resurrection this incident took place. However, the disciples have had time to journey from Jerusalem back to Galilee.

Sea of Tiberias. Tiberias was a city founded on the shore of the Sea of Galilee in A.D. 20 by Herod. By the time this Gospel was written, this new name for the Sea of Galilee had become well-known. At the close of Mark's Gospel (Mark 16:7), the angel tells the women that Jesus is going ahead of his disciples into Galilee and they are to follow him there.

21:2 On this occasion seven of the disciples are together. Five are identified. The sons of Zebedee are James and John (Mark 1:19–20). The two anonymous disciples may be unnamed since they have not been previously featured in the Gospel of John. Nathanael was mentioned as one of the earliest followers of Jesus (John 1:45–51), but his name does not appear in any list of the Twelve (e.g., Mark 3:16–19). A common guess is that he is the Bartholomew whose name does appear.

21:3 *I'm going out to fish.* Peter, along with his brother Andrew and James and John, were fishermen when Jesus called them (Mark 1:16–20). As such, they may be returning to their trade. It is certainly not surprising as they wait for the Lord in Galilee (as they have been instructed) that they should decide to go fishing. But, in fact, this action on their part has another, metaphoric dimension to it. When Jesus called these four men to follow him he promised them: "I will make you fishers of men" (Mark 1:17). So far, this promise had not been fulfilled (nor could it be prior to Jesus' redeeming death and resurrection). On their own, the disciples are not going to become these sort of fishermen. They have labored all night and come up empty. But then Jesus comes and instructs them how to fish (v. 6), and they become successful. This is a vivid prediction of what is ahead for the disciples. They will be empowered by Jesus to become successful fishers of men.

that night. Much of the fishing on the Sea of Galilee took place at night. Fishermen carried blazing torches that enabled them to spot schools of fish and sometimes drew fish to the surface. But this reference may also have a metaphoric sense. The disciples are still "in the dark" when it comes to what the risen Christ wants of them. At dawn they will see Jesus on shore and he will give them direction. In John 13:30 the same double meaning is found. Judas leaves the Last Supper in order to betray Jesus. John notes: "And it was night."

21:4 *the disciples did not realize that it was Jesus.* There are two other resurrection appearances in which Jesus is not immediately recognized (Luke 24:15–16; John 20:14). Paul speaks of the resurrected body as having a different type of splendor than the normal body (1 Cor. 15:40–42). Whether these men failed to recognize him because it was still early and therefore somewhat dark or if there was some type of transformation in Jesus' appearance that caused them to be unable to

immediately identify him is not told, but verse 12 indicates that the latter is likely.

21:6 *they were unable to haul the net in because of the large number of fish.* The lack of success after fishing all night, the call to throw in the net one more time, and the particular emphasis on the response of Peter are all very similar to the miracle recorded at the beginning of Jesus' ministry in Luke 5:1–11. The repetition of such a miracle would underscore the emphasis which Jesus made at that time that, with him, they would be very successful as "fishers of men." This particular miracle at this time would have special meaning to Peter whose threefold denial of Christ must have plagued him with doubts about his ability to be an apostle.

21:7 *the disciple whom Jesus loved.* This is thought to be John, the author of the Gospel.

It is the Lord! As Jesus' voice opened Mary's eyes to recognize him (John 20:16), so here the enormous catch of fish revealed him to the beloved disciple. It is significant that in all the resurrection appearances Jesus is called by this divine title (John 20:18,25). Just as Jesus had said in John 8:28, the glorification that would be his through his death and resurrection sealed the belief of his followers in his divine identity.

he wrapped his outer garment around him. This refers to Peter tucking up his fisherman's smock so he could swim to shore.

21:9 *a fire of burning coals.* It is significant that the same word used in John 18:18 to describe the fire around which Peter was standing when he betrayed Jesus is used here to describe the fire at which Jesus will draw Peter back into the company of his disciples (see John 21:15–17). These are the only two uses of this term in the New Testament.

21:11 *153.* Although there have been many attempts from earliest times on to find a symbolic meaning for this number, there is no agreement whatsoever about what it might be! It appears that this is an instance of the author simply reporting the facts about a phenomenal event.

21:12 *None of the disciples dared ask him, "Who are you?"* In light of the confession of the beloved disciple in verse 7, it is difficult to know what the author intends by this statement. It somewhat parallels the experience of the disciples in Matthew 28:17 where, in the context of another resurrection appearance, some of his followers were still unsure about him. On the other hand, the author may mean that their certainty about who he was meant they no longer had to ask this question. This is the question that had been asked of Jesus in various ways throughout the Gospel of John (John 4:12; 7:12,26,40–41; 8:25; 9:35–36). In contrast to the confusion the disciples experienced previously (see John 16:17–18), now their understanding of his identity and mission is complete.

breakfast. The Jesus that they met was no disembodied spirit. He had a body. They could see him and hear him and eat with him. He had hands and feet that allowed him to kindle a fire on the beach. Jesus had been resurrected bodily. He had conquered death.

21:13 *Jesus came, took the bread and gave it to them.* In the Gospel of John there is no account of the Last Supper. However, the words used here are very similar to words used at the Last Supper (see Mark 14:22). Furthermore, the bread and the fish are reminiscent of the feeding of the five thousand where there is a clear parallel to Communion (see John 6:11 and the notes for Mark 6:41 in Unit 5). It is via participation in this meal that the disciples come to recognize who Jesus is. A similar thing happens in Luke 24:30–31. The disciples on the road to Emmaus meet a mysterious stranger whom they discover—in the breaking of the bread—to be Jesus. Down through the ages the church continues to celebrate the Lord's Supper in remembrance of Jesus (1 Cor. 11:23–26). So too the church continues to recognize the presence of Jesus in the breaking of the bread.

21:14 *the third time.* This is the third resurrection account described in John's Gospel (see John 20:19–23 and 24–29). Altogether, some 12 appearances are described or alluded to in the New Testament. Jesus appeared to Mary Magdalene (Mark 16:9; John 20:11–18), to the women (Matt. 28:9–10), to Cleopas and his companion (Luke 24:13–35), to Simon Peter (Luke 24:34; 1 Cor. 15:5), to all the disciples except Thomas (John 20:19–23), to all the disciples (John 20:24–29), to the seven disciples here at the Sea of Galilee (John 21:1–14), to the disciples on a mountain in Galilee (Matt. 28:16–20), to more than 500 (1 Cor. 15:6), to James, the brother of Jesus (1 Cor. 15:7), to the disciples on Olivet at the Ascension (Acts 1:4–11), and to Paul on his way to Damascus (Acts 9:3–7; 22:6–10; 26:12–18; 1 Cor. 9:1; 15:8). The post-resurrection appearances are important for a number of reasons. For one thing, they are part of the proof of Jesus' resurrection (along with the fact of the empty tomb, the collapsed and empty grave clothes, etc.). Second, they show that Jesus had conquered death. He was not simply a disembodied spirit who appeared as a ghost-like figure, a hallucination, or a vision. He was real and had a body. Third, they describe how it was that the disciples learned of their mission. Fourth, it was the encounter with the living Jesus that changed the disciples from frightened men in hiding to bold witnesses who changed the world. Finally, the post-resurrection appearances show to all of us that Jesus is still alive and thus we can enter into a personal relationship with him even today.